I0114858

THE CAREY / CARY FAMILY

RESEARCHING, CONNECTING AND SHARING FAMILY HISTORY

E. Niel Carey
Managing Editor

Copyright © 2019 by individual article authors
Edited and curated by E. Niel Carey

All rights reserved.

ISBN 978-1-62806-251-9 (print | hardcover)

Library of Congress Control Number 2019916021

Published by Salt Water Media
29 Broad Street, Suite 104
Berlin, MD 21811
www.saltwatermedia.com

Salt Water
MEDIA

TABLE OF CONTENTS

SECTION 3
SUPPORTING AND STRENGTHENING
THE CAREY/CARY FAMILY ORGANIZATION

PREFACE

The purpose of this book is to provide a permanent record of the development and achievements of the Carey/Cary Family organization over the past quarter century and to recognize its leaders--Carey/Cary family members and friends--who have worked creatively and diligently to make this happen. While many of these leaders have full time work and family responsibilities, they agreed to write the chapters of this book During this twenty-five year period our family group has become organized with a constitution and by-laws; planned and conducted twenty-five successful annual reunions with participants from nineteen states; conducted and shared family research; published and distributed a Carey/Cary Family newsletter; encouraged DNA testing by family members and others; developed a Carey/Cary Family website: www.careycary.org; and developed productive relationships with Carey's United Methodist Church and the Nabb Research Center on Delmarva History and Culture at Salisbury University. National and state archives, the Church of Jesus Christ of Latter-Day Saints (LDS) and its local family research libraries, and state and local historical societies have been valuable sources of information and support.

The book's front cover features the Carey/Cary coat of arms. The back cover features sketch art of Carey's United Methodist Church by Anne Ward's sister, Barbara D. Redman.

The book has three sections: The first tells of the beginning and organization of our family group; the second section includes summaries of family history that family members and others have prepared; and the third summarizes the development of relationships with supportive organizations as well as our own support systems such as the www.careycary.org website. Don Ward's comprehensive chapter in the second section summarizing Don's extensive family research and his leadership in encouraging Car-

Carey / Cary Family Reunion, September 10, 1994

Back row: Brian Phillips, John Pfotzer, Bill Carey, Diana Nichols, Gerry Nichols, Lee Dobson, Leroy Taylor, Jos. Doughtery, Lottie Doughtery, Don Law

Next row: Lida Wells, Marty Monroe, Jean Masche

Next row: Richard Weiant, Linda Meade, Barbara Phillips, Franklin Ross, Hase Carey, Mak Carey, Dr. Asher Carey, Ellen Howard, Jacque Law

Next row: Erma Weiant, Oneida Monroe, Laura McDonald, Vaugh Carey, Ina Carey Hastings, Roberta Taylor, Pauline Carey, Rick Carey

Front row: Helen Carey, Pansy Wilso, Niel Carey, Jo Cary, Rodger Cary, Barbara Carey

ey's Church support of the Carey/Cary Family organization is an interesting bridge to the third section. In addition, chapters obviously reflect the valuable contributions of the authors and their varying personal styles of communicating and writing. These differences reflect the diversity of talents, accomplishments and philanthropy of Carey/Cary Family members and friends.

Families provide the strength, creativity and productivity of our communities and our society. We hope that by sharing the story of the Carey/Cary Family organization we will encourage other families to do the same. Helen and I will contribute the cost of publishing this book as a means of celebrating our 61st wedding anniversary on August 16, 2019, and of expressing our appreciation for the support and contributions of our many Carey/Cary Family members and friends. Special thanks to our publisher, Stephanie Fowler and her staff at SaltWater Media for their talent and skill in helping us produce this important, attractive book on schedule.

- E. Niel Carey, President
Carey/Cary Family organization

Richard G. (Rick) Carey, Vice President; Helen S. Carey, Treasurer and Newsletter Editor; Barbara C. Philips, Secretary; Barbara Carey, Director of Public relations; Sean Gilson, Website and DNA Project Director

Carey / Cary Family Reunion, October 20-21, 2018

Left to right, 1st row: Laura C. McDonald, Helen Carey, Niel Carey, Dorothy Carey, Barbara C. Phillips

2nd row: Mary Garland, Peggy Johnston, Kenneth Johnston, Rick Carey, Neill Carey, Jim Joyce, Jane Gardner, Barbara Carey, Marian Bower, Bryan Phillips

3rd row: John Garland, Terry & Steve Carey, G. Paul Carey, Nancy Carey, Gary Gardner, Don Ward, Dr. Creston Long, Aaron Homer, Mike Hitch

SECTION I

GETTING STARTED AND GETTING ORGANIZED

CHAPTER I

THE CAREY/CARY FAMILY: ITS BEGINNING AND GROWTH
- E. NIEL CAREY -

The decision to publish the Carey/Cary Family book--as a means of providing a permanent record of the beginning and growth of the Carey/Cary Family organization--was made at the twenty-fifth Carey/Cary Family reunion. From the very first reunion when those attending decided that the family group would not be limited to one Carey/Carey blood line, and when it was decided that the group would be known as the Carey/Cary Family, it was clear that the family group was inclusive and action-oriented. Subsequent reunions and family activities would reinforce this notion. The decision to write and publish the Carey/Cary Family book was based on the wealth of genealogical information gathered and shared at the reunions, the increased information about the various Carey/Cary family lines, and the interaction and friendships that have developed at the reunions and from family communication.

The twenty-fifth Carey/Cary Family reunion was held on October 20, 2018, at Salisbury University's Nabb Research Center on Delmarva History and Culture and with a special church service at the Carey's United Methodist Church on 21 October. The reunion was very successful. After registration and lunch Dr. Creston Long, Nabb Center Director, welcomed the group. Niel Carey commented on the significance of the reunion, completing a quarter century of growth of the

Carey/Cary Family organization. He also extended the greetings of several key family members who were unable to attend including Alfred Carey, Diane Hansen and Sean Gilson. He then introduced the program which included presentations by Mike Hitch, Don Ward, Creston Long, Peggy Johnston and Helen Carey.

Following the program, in the business session, the possibility of publishing a Carey/Cary Family book was discussed. Prior to the reunion Niel had discussed (with our officers and several family members) the idea of a joint effort in writing a book which could provide a permanent record of the organization and growth of the Carey/Cary Family; responses had been positive. Also, several individuals were asked if they would be willing to write a chapter for the book and their responses were also positive. When this information was shared at the reunion, there was considerable interest and encouragement to proceed. A time frame of having a first draft of the book by October 2019 was suggested, and Niel agreed to provide suggestions for sections of the book for further discussion.

The proposed sections would include an introductory section which would provide information about how the first reunion was organized and how Carey/Cary Family organization grew out of that reunion. Rick Carey and Niel agreed to write the chapters for this section. The second section would include chapters written by family members who have done family research on the Carey/Cary Family. Diane Hansen, Tony Carey, Neill Carey, Rex Carey, Peggy Johnston, Don Ward, Ed Carey and Helen Carey have agreed to write chapters for this section. Other members are considering writing a chapter. The third section would include chapters on means of communication with family members or those interested in the Carey/Cary Family, sharing family research and supporting Carey/Cary Family activities and programs. These would include the Carey Family Newsletter, the CareyCary website, the DNA project, and the involvement of Carey's Church and the Nabb Research center.

In the book, the chapter authors will share a summary of the research they have done or explain how their activities or work has actively supported the Carey/Cary Family organization. The chapters will describe the impressive progress the family organization has made since the first reunion was held in the Fenwick Inn, Ocean City, MD, area on September 9, 1994.

The first reunion grew out of two events. First, in 1976 Helen and Niel and their young daughters Laura and Rebecca went on a sightseeing auto trip to the west coast in the summer of 1976. On the eastbound portion of the trip they spent the night in Cheyenne, WY. While there, their daughters discovered a Carey Street sign and aked to have their picture taken beside it. Later, when visiting the state capital, Niel noticed a prominent display featuring Governor Joseph Maull Carey, Wyoming governor in the 1880s. The display included the information that Governor Carey was born in Milton, DE, which is somewhat near the Bishopville, MD, area where some of Niel's paternal ancestors had lived. Since his wife Helen was already interested in researching her Simmons family history, he suggested that she research his Carey family to determine a possible relationship with Governor Carey.

To digress, after returning to Maryland, Niel gathered and read information about Joseph Maull Carey's impressive career as a public servant, elected official and successful businessman. Joseph Maull Carey was born in Milton, DE, in

1845, educated in public and private schools, attended Union College in Schenectady, NY, and received his law degree from the University of Pennsylvania in 1867. He was active in Ulysses S. Grant's presidential campaign, and after Grant was elected president, he appointed Mr. Carey as the first U.S. Attorney for the Territory of Wyoming. After two years in the position he resigned in order to serve as a judge of the Wyoming Territorial Supreme Court. From 1871-1876, he served as a member of the Republican National Committee and from 1881-1985 he served as Mayor of Cheyenne. He was appointed the Territory of Wyoming's Delegate to the U.S. House of Representatives and took the oath of office in December 1885. Even though he had no vote, he was a very active legislator. While he introduced and supported many bills, he introduced, defended and finally secured passage of legislation making Wyoming a state. That legislation also gave Wyoming women the right to vote, the first state to do so. In a later comment, Mr. Carey stated that "Suffrage is the fountain of power, giving women the strength to protect themselves. It places in their hands additional influence to secure a place and means of employment..." President Harrison signed the legislation making Wyoming the forty-fourth State of the Union on July 10, 1890.

After Wyoming became a state, the Wyoming legislature selected Joseph Maull Carey as the first U. S. Senator from the state. As Senator, he became involved in several legislative issues including a law making silver the basis for U.S. currency which he opposed, tariff legislation which he supported in order to protect Wyoming jobs, and legislation transferring federal land to the states known as the *Carey Act*. However, his stand on the silver legislation caused his loss of Wyoming voter support and most likely resulted in his defeat for a second term. He later said that as an elected official he would always vote his convictions, even if it resulted in his defeat.

Mr. Carey made a political comeback in 1910. When he did not receive the Republican nomination for Governor, he was nominated and elected as a Democrat, serving from 1911 to 1915. During that time he and several other governors joined with Theodore Roosevelt to form the Progressive Party.

Joseph Maull Carey was also a successful land owner, rancher and business man. He was the President of the Wyoming Development Company and the Wheatland Industrial Company and served as the President of the Wyoming Stock Growers Association. He is in the Cowboy Hall of Fame. He served as a member of the Cheyenne School Board and as a Trustee of the University of Wyoming.

After a life of public service at the local, state and national levels and of business Joseph Maull Carey died at his home in Cheyenne on February 5, 1924. It is quite appropriate that Joseph Maull Carey's life story of service and leadership was a motivating factor in the formation of the Carey/Cary Family organization.

Members of Joseph Maull Carey's family have been involved with and supportive of the Carey/Cary Family organization. Prior to his death Helen Carey corresponded with Charles D. Carey, Jr., who provided valuable family information. Niel and Helen Carey met and communicated with his wife, Margaret, now deceased, who attended the Carey Reunion service at Carey's Church' They have also communicated and met with their daughter, Ellison Carey, who made a presentation on the Joseph Maull Carey family line at the 2009 Carey/Cary Family reunion. In addition, Helen and Niel also established contact with the sister of Charles David Carey, Jr., Louise Bon of CA, deceased.

The second event in respect to the organizing a family organization resulted from a phone message Niel received. The phone message was from a Richard Carey, and asked if Niel was one of the Careys from the Eastern Shore of Maryland. Niel returned the call, and discovered that Richard – he preferred Rick – and he were second cousins. Rick indicated that he was a member of the LDS Church and was interested in Carey family history. Niel mentioned that Helen had started researching the family history, and jokingly mentioned that they should have a family reunion to share the family information they had gathered. Rick agreed enthusiastically with the suggestion, so they agreed to pursue the idea.

After agreeing that a family reunion was a good idea, Rick and Niel then discussed and decided on a time and a location and compiled a list of family members to invite. They asked those they contacted to spread the word about the reunion and were pleased at the enthusiastic response. Rick had a good network, including internet connections.

Niel's father, the late Vaughn Carey, suggested that they contact Carey's United Methodist Church and explore attendance at their service as part of the reunion. He knew Ralph Dorey, a Carey's Church leader through the Ruritans and Niel and Vaughn met with him to discuss the idea. Ralph was very receptive, but suggested that they contact Don Ward to make the arrangements. Niel contacted Don who was very enthusiastic about recognizing the Carey/Cary family at a Sunday service. This started and continued the warm welcome at Carey's

Church, along with an ongoing and very positive relationship with Don and Anne Ward and their family.

The first reunion was a successful and interesting event. In the discussion the group accepted Rodger Cary's suggestion that we indicate the inclusiveness of our family group by referring to the family organization as the Carey/Cary Family. The group agreed that that we should adopt the Carey/Cary Family name, that we form a family organization, and that we have an annual reunion. Officers were nominated and elected: Niel was elected president; Rick, vice president; Margaret Sherkey secretary; and Barbara Carey treasurer. Helen agreed to develop a newsletter, and Niel agreed to draft a constitution and by-laws for the officers to review. The enthusiastic discussion and interaction in the first reunion provided the vision and organizational foundation for our family organization.

In the years following the first reunion, the Carey/Cary Family organization developed in a manner that enabled its members to communicate, to continue to conduct family research, and to share that research. Helen Carey edited and produced the *Carey/Cary Family Newsletter* which became an important communications tool for sharing family research and other information related to the Carey/Cary Family. Family member Sean Gilson recommended the formation of a Carey/Cary Family website and agreed to develop and manage it. Sean later pointed to the importance of DNA testing to family research, and he agreed to help family members understand the importance of DNA testing and to encourage their participation. Family members including Diane Hansen and the late Jan Pullins, Tony Carey, Ellison Carey, Sean Gilson, Dr. Neill Carey, the late David Carey, Ed Carey, Ron Blevins, Barbara Philips and Linda Meade and others shared information about their family research and techniques to preserve family history and lore at the annual reunions, in the family newsletter and/or on the family website: www.careycary.org. About fourteen years later, when it was decided that the website would be the primary communications tool, the newsletter was discontinued and the existing newsletters were bound and copies provided to several libraries and organizations including the LDS library in Salt Lake City, the Carey Family Research Room at the Nabb Research Center at Salisbury University, the public library at Carey, OH, The Duke University Library, and the Carey Family Center at the MD Historical Society in Baltimore. The newsletters are available on the Carey/Cary website, www.careycary.org.

The annual family reunions have provided family members and others with the opportunity to come together, to share information, and to discuss the importance of becoming aware of and preserving family history. While the reunions have been held in various places, for the past several years the reunion has been held at the Nabb Research Center on Delmarva History and Culture at Salisbury University. This arrangement grew out of Niel's service as a member and chair of the Nabb Board of Directors and the strong interest and enthusiastic support of the previous director Dr. Ray Thompson, and the current director, Dr. Creston Long. The Nabb Center has provided an excellent meeting facility, and the Nabb Center staff-- including Donna Messick and Aaron Horner--have provided outstanding logistical and technical support. Reunion attendees have come primarily from Delaware, Maryland and Virginia, but also from seventeen states including Texas, California, Oregon, New Mexico, North Carolina, Pennsylvania, Georgia, Florida, Indiana, Arizona. All attendees have received the very attractive Carey/Cary reunion packet featuring the Carey/Cary coat of arms provided by Barbara Carey.

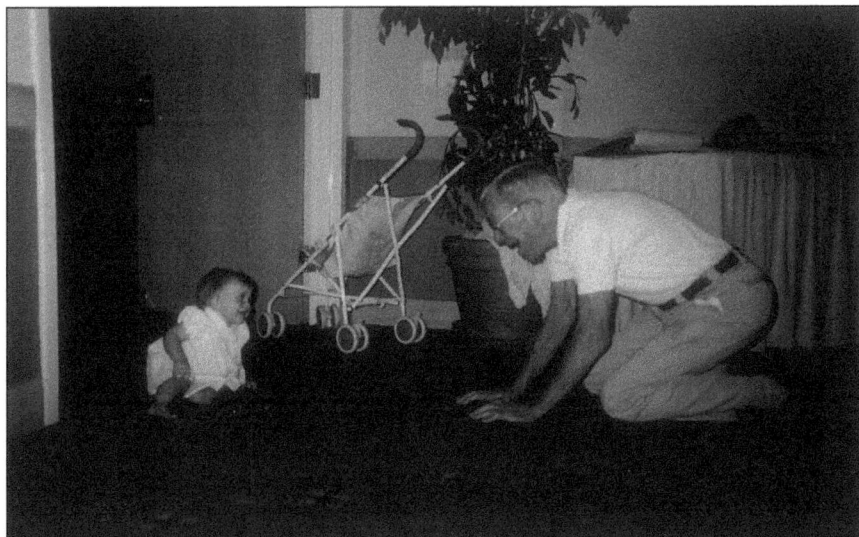

Carey McDonald and Hase Carey - 1995 Carey / Cary Reunion

The reunions, the newsletters and the website have encouraged and enabled an expanding network of extended family members to communicate, share information and in some cases discover related family ties. Don Ward and Niel discovered common Jones family heritage and Dr. Neill Carey and Niel realized that they have common heritage in both Carey and Dykes lines. The family network has extended across the country and beyond. Several years ago, following a contact from Rick Carey's network, Helen and Niel contacted Bob and Joy Carey in southern England, and visited with them during their travels to England to research the Carey/Cary family in the Torquay and Bristol areas. Most recently, as a result of DNA testing, Dennis and Kareen Carey of the Tampa, FL, area contacted Helen and shared a wealth of Carey family research.

In order to recognize and also preserve the wealth of information and family ties resulting from the Carey/Cary reunions; the family research gathered and shared; the extensive network of family members as well as other benefits, this book has been organized and published. The book is an impressive team effort with the chapters written by individuals who have been actively involved in and supportive of the Carey/Cary Family organization. Deep appreciation is extended to the chapter authors who have contributed in so many ways to the Carey/Cary family network, and have contributed even further by writing a chapter for this book.

- E. Niel Carey

Co-Founder and President, Carey/Cary Family organization; Graduate, Pittsville High School, B.S., STC (Now Salisbury U), MEd, U of Maryland; Teacher, Counselor, Dept. Chair, Baltimore County; MD State Coordinator of Career Education; Executive Director Emeritus, National Career Development Association; Member Emeritus, Nabb Center Board of Directors

Chapter 2

Starting the Carey/Cary Family Organization
- Richard G. (Rick) Carey -

I started researching my Carey genealogy shortly after becoming a member of the Church of Jesus Christ of Latter Day Saints in February 1984. Most of my research was centered on records, mostly microfilm and microfiche at The Family History Center of the Church in Wilmington, Delaware. I volunteered at the Center during this time. There I met Alvin Carey who lived in the Wilmington area who was researching the Carey family also and we shared information. During the Civil War there were four Carey brothers who served in the Union Army. One was Alvin Carey's grandfather. The Delaware Genealogical society had a picture of the Carey brothers which was displayed at their location in Wilmington for several months. I also contacted many of my relatives in southern Delaware and in Maryland. My success was limited. My father, the youngest member of his family, passed away in 1981. He knew very little about Carey history. I did talk with him about family a few times but he had little knowledge or information that would have been helpful. He said he was told by relatives as a young boy that we were of English heritage. He was born on 22 October 1908 in Bishopville, Worcester County, Maryland.

Computers were becoming popular around this time period so I placed a few requests on line looking for anyone who was researching the genealogy of Careys in Delaware, Maryland and the Eastern shore. When you have success in researching family names, dates and places there are times answers to questions come from unexpected sources. I'm a firm believer in divine intervention when trying to uncover deceased ancestors. (No pun intended) They want to be found and not forgotten by us. Of this I'm sure. After a short time I received an email from one Rodger Cary who lived in upstate New York telling me his father was born in Worcester County, Maryland, and he too was researching the Carey/Cary family. He included in his comments that I was the first Carey he had met on line. We exchanged family information and stayed in contact from that time on. Rodger also told me his father was instrumental in helping design the jet engine on the B-52 Bomber. Another gentleman I met on line was Wolf (Carey) Wilson I believe he lived in Arizona. He told me his father David Wilson was adopted but was really a Carey by birth. David later attended several reunions and has since passed away. He was an excellent genealogist and shared his research with our organization.

I also went to Snow Hill, Maryland, during this time period with a friend from church who was doing research on the Hearn family. His name was Rodney Hearn and he had roots in Sussex County, Delaware, and Worcester County, Maryland. He was a great help as he found the telephone number of a gentleman in New York state that was posted on a bulletin board at the Snow Hill library in Worcester County, asking anyone who was looking for Carey information from the Eastern Shore to contact him. His name was Franklin Ross who was connected to the Careys through his mother. Franklin shared his information with me and our organization, attending many reunions with his wife before they passed away a few years ago.

There were other researchers with whom I talked and exchanged information, gaining some great advice on record research. But the real break came when I called Niel Carey in Ellicott City, Maryland. This is where my research took on an air of excitement. At the time I was working night shift at the General Motors Assembly plant in Wilmington, Delaware. As I wrote previously I believe our ancestors want to be found and we sometimes receive information where and when we least expect it. One night I had a dream I was driving on the interstate and passed a sign that read Ellicott City. This did not have any meaning to me except my wife Barbara and I attended the Washington Temple of The Church of Jesus Christ of Latter Day Saints several times a year and I remember seeing an exit for Ellicott City just south of Baltimore. I could not stop thinking about the dream. So one afternoon I called Maryland information and ask the operator if she would check for any Carey listings in the Ellicott City area. She found two numbers so I wrote them down. I don't remember their first names but I called the first number without success, no answer. I called the second number and a very nice lady answered. I told her who I was and I was doing genealogy research on the Carey family. She was very helpful but said her husband was of Scandinavian ancestry she thought. She offered to use her phone book and see if there were any Careys listed. She did so and Niel Carey and one other Carey were listed. I wrote the numbers down and thanked her for her help. Just before we ended our conversation she said I should call this Niel Carey he might be able to help you. Why she offered that advice I will probably never know. At this point I decided to call Niel Carey as suggested. I dialed the number and was connected to an answering machine. A very friendly female voice said no one was available to take the call but to leave a message and phone number and the call would be returned. I might add she also repeated the message in Spanish. I left a message directed to Niel Carey as follows. "My name is Richard Carey (Rick) and I'm researching the Carey family. Would you be related to a John Franklin Carey who at one time was a Methodist minister on the Eastern Shore. If you know anything about this family I would love to speak with you."

When I returned from work that evening my wife told me that Niel Carey had called about a message I left on his answering machine. I called him back the next day and we realized we were second cousins. Niel suggested that we meet for lunch in the near future to discuss sharing information I had and that his wife Helen had. She too was doing research on the Careys and her own Simmons line. Niel and Helen, my wife Barbara and I met at the Columbus Inn in Wilmington in early 1993. We discussed the family and Niel suggested that we might be able to put a family reunion together sometime in the future. We all agreed that the idea was worth looking into. We also decided that we would come up with ideas to share and voice them at another meeting in the near future. In late 1993 or early 1994 we met again and decided, after sharing thoughts and ideas, that a reunion would take place in September of the same year. The preparations begin. We decided to put a list of names together of people to invite. Invitation was by telephone, e-mail and regular mail. Niel secured reservations with The Fenwick Inn, Fenwick, Delaware, and we were on our way to what we hoped would be a successful reunion.

Another source of information I would like to mention are our Carey/Cary newsletters. It was decided at the first reunion

Helen, Barbara, Vaughn, Niel, and Rick Carey
1995 Carey/Cary Family Reunion

that maybe we should publish an annual or semi-annual newsletter. This seemed like a great idea and Helen Carey graciously agreed to look into it. Not long after the first newsletter was
born. Several years later my wife and I planned a trip to Salt
Lake City, Utah. When I told Niel and Helen where we were
going, Niel suggested we take copies of all newsletters printed
thus far to the Family History Library which we intended to
visit. Helen packaged the letters and we hand-carried them to
Salt Lake City, where they we happily accepted. As additional
newsletters were published, they were mailed to the Library.

Finally, after fourteen years of publishing newsletter, it was
decided to discontinue the project and take advantage of our
web site (www.careycary.org) for communication. Thanks to
Sean Gilson, all newsletters were archived on the site. Also, a
bound copy of all newsletters were shipped to the library in
Salt Lake City. The bound volume is titled *Carey/Cary Family
Newsletters A Collection of Family History and News.*

- Richard G. (Rick) Carey

Co-Founder and Vice President, Carey/Cary Family organization; Born: 1946 Wilmington, New Castle County, Delaware; Attended Newark, New Castle County, Delaware Schools; Served 2 years in US Army; 1 Year in Viet Nam; Retired from General Motors with 30 years service; Currently serving as Co-Director with my wife at the FHC in Wilmington, Delaware; Married to Barbara Philbrick; 3 Children, 10 Grandchildren, 3 Great-Grandchildren

CHAPTER 3

BUILDING, STRENGTHENING
AND ENJOYING FAMILY TIES
- E. NIEL CAREY -

Helen and our daughters stopped in Cheyenne, Wyoming, as part of a trip to the west coast and learned that a Joseph Maull Carey, Governor of Wyoming was from Milton, Delaware. In jest, I suggested that Helen, with her interest in family history, determine if we were related... That probably reinforced Helen's desire to expand her genealogy skills and certainly increased my interest in family history. Over time, Rick Carey's phone call asking about Eastern Shore Careys resulted in our Carey/Cary Family reunions, increased our involvement and support of the Nabb Research Center, and strengthened our family ties.

In this chapter I want to highlight the friendships and the very valuable relationships of several of the extended family members and friends who have added to our family information. These have been major factors in forming and strengthening the Carey/Cary Family organization. A few of these good friends include Don and Anne Ward, Bud and Sue Hudson and Bud's father, Charlie, Dr. Neill and Nancy Carey, Sean Gilson, Mike Hitch, Diane Hansen, Tony and Eleanor Carey, Ed Carey, Ellison Carey, Cecily Hintzen, Rex and Janice Carey, Peggy Johnston and her husband Kenneth (Helen's cousin), my cousin Rick Carey and his wife, Barbara, my cousin

Barbara Carey Phillips and her husband Bryan, and my wife Helen Carey.

When Rick Carey and I agreed that we should plan a Carey Family reunion in order to share family history information, my father Vaughn Carey suggested that we might want to involve Carey's United Methodist Church near Millsboro, DE. He agreed to contact Ralph Dorey, a long-time member of Carey's Church. When we met with Ralph, he strongly recommended that we communicate with Don Ward, an active leader in the Carey's Church community. Don was immediately interested in having Carey's Church be a part of the reunion. He mentioned that his and Anne's home is on land owned by Elijah Carey who contributed the land for Carey's Church. He said he would suggest a special church service followed by a luncheon and that he would discuss this with Carey's Church Board of Trustees. The trustees enthusiastically supported Don's suggestion and, as a result, the Carey's service and luncheon has become an important part of the Carey/Cary Family Reunion.

Don's background is impressive. After retiring from a successful career in education as a teacher and administrator in Sussex County schools, Don started a business as a land developer and home builder in Sussex County. He and his son Drew have a successful business building homes and developing communities. Their reputation in the community is evidence of their success. Don is very active in various community activities and Don and Drew, their wives and Don's sister, Berta Smith, have important leadership roles in Carey's Church and Camp. As we worked with Don to set the date and other details of the Carey's Church service, we got to know him and valued his knowledge and leadership in the Church and its community. We have become good friends and have discovered that we have common ancestry in the Jones family line which developed in and around the MD/DE line south of Carey's Church.

Don has been interested in and supportive of the Carey/Cary Family reunion. He has consistently provided interesting and valuable information related to the Carey/Cary family, including information about the formation of Carey's Church and Camp. He is also working with Dr. Long at the Nabb Research Center to gather oral histories of individuals in Don's community. This information is provided in greater detail in Don's chapter in this book.

The Edward H. Nabb Research Center on Delmarva History and Culture has a highly capable and helpful staff and an extensive collection of books, records and artifacts from Delaware, Maryland and Virginia. Helen and I heard of the Center's existence and found it to have a wealth of records and information related to the Carey/Cary Family. Dr. Ray Thompson, co-founder and previous director, and Dr. Creston Long, its current director, graciously invited the Carey/Cary Family to meet at the Center. We enthusiastically accepted that invitation for the past several years and found the Center's staff to be very supportive and helpful. Donna Messick has arranged for the meeting room, including technical support. Aaron Horner and/or other staff have been available to assist family members in their research. Mike Hitch, current Chair of the Nabb Center Board of Directors, has been a valuable source of information, especially about land grants related to the Carey/Cary family. His chapter provides information and perspective about his family research.

As a member and previous chair of the Nabb Center Board

of Directors, I chaired the Nabb committee which developed the Center's first strategic plan. Dr. Ray Thompson and Nabb staff published the plan, which included attractive as well as meaningful pictures from the Center's collection. I was honored to be named Emeritus Board of Directors member. Helen and I were pleased to endow the Carey Family Research room in the Center.

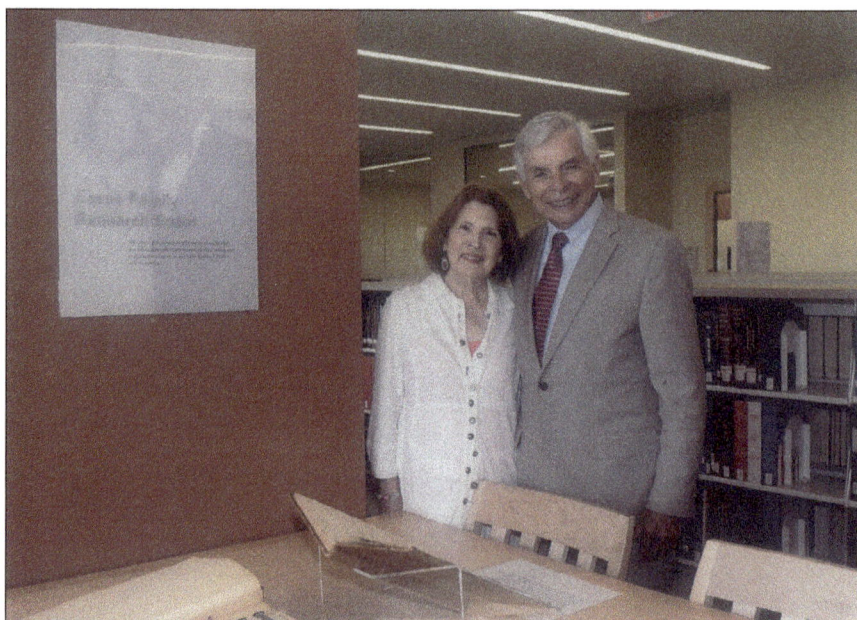

Niel and Helen Carey at the dedication of the Carey Family Research Room at the Nabb center – October 2016

After Mr. Charlie Hudson of nearby Gumboro, DE, bought the farm that Helen and I had purchased from my Aunt Ina (Carey) we got to know him and his wife and became very good friends. After his son Bud and his wife Sue moved to the farm, they grew corn and soybeans, while also raising broiler chickens and hogs. Fortunately, they have been very successful. Bud now owns or leases several hundred acres of farmland and has a fleet of trucks, tractors, combines, an irrigation system, other equipment, and appropriate tools to operate his extensive farm acreage. Sue had a sideline of raising and selling chihuahua pups. They were very good neighbors to my parents, Vaughn and Doris Carey, who lived on the adjoining farm. As my parents grew older, Bud tilled Dad's farm, Sue would often take them food, and Dad and Charlie simply enjoyed getting together and talking about various topics.

At one point, Charlie may have realized that he has Jones ancestors, and Dad showed Charlie and Bud where his grandfather Jones resided. My maternal grandfather (Jones) owned much of the land that Bud now farms. Charlie thought highly of Dad, and when he recently acquired copies of the Jones Family book, he has been pleased to realize that we are distantly related. For me, this was an example of how people can discuss family history and sometimes discover family ties of which they had been unaware. After my parents died, my sister Susan and I were very willing and pleased to sell the remainder of my parents' farm to Bud and Sue. Susan and Bud also worked with the leaders of Line Church, my parents' church, to develop a Healing Garden at the church utilizing the smoke house which Bud transported from my parents' farm to the church.

Helen and I met Dr. Neill Carey and his wife Nancy at a Salisbury University function, when he was introduced as "the other Niel Carey". Neill and Nancy are long-time residents of the Newtown Historic District in Salisbury. Both had careers in Laboratory Medicine. Neill is a clinical chemist, and he has practiced as a professor, manager, and consultant in that field. Nancy was a laboratory supervisor. They are active supporters of Salisbury University and of Public Radio Delmarva. Both have served on the Newtown Historic Commission. Neill is also an active supporter of the maintenance and preservation of Parsons Cemetery in Salisbury as well as the Chipman Center. As Neill and Nancy became active members of the Carey/Cary Family organization, he enthusiastically shared his knowledge of family history. At one of the family reunions, Neill and my cousin Barbara Phillips created an interesting and entertaining presentation on the two Sam Careys of Salisbury. Neill's father was Sam Carey, a manager of WBOC-TV. Barbara's father was the other Sam Carey, my father's older brother. Uncle Sam was very helpful in my admission process at Salisbury State College and later helped me obtain my first career position as an agent for the Home Beneficial Insurance Company.

As it evolved DNA tests for the two Careys (Neill and Niel) indicate a common Carey heritage. We also have a Dykes' family connection. Research has determined that our maternal great-great grandfather was the same, Michael Dykes in Somerset Co., MD. . Neill's chapter in this book provides additional information about his family research and connections.

Sean Gilson became a member of the Carey/Cary Family organization to research his mother's Carey family connection. After he suggested the advantages of a family website, he agreed to develop and manage one. As a result, the Carey/Cary Family website, www.careycary.org , has become a valuable communication tool for our organization. Sean also became interested in DNA testing as an important genealogy tool.

Sean presented information about DNA testing at a Carey/Cary Family reunion and later agreed to develop and manage a family DNA project to encourage family members to participate in DNA testing. As a result of this project, an increasing number of family members have been tested and shared the results. Sean has recently moved from the east coast to Arizona, has increased work responsibilities, and he and Amy have two very young sons, but he continues to manage the website and promote the DNA testing process.

Several family members and friends have researched and shared a great deal of information about the Carey family or their Carey/Cary line. Diane Hansen and her cousin, the late Jan Pullins, often traveled from their homes in Indiana to the Eastern Shore area to gather information from archives, libraries and cemeteries. They shared detailed information (and entertaining experiences) at Carey/Cary Family reunions. Their Carey family research was extensive, including the migration of family members to the mid-west. Their knowledge of the Eastern Shore geography and history was impressive.

Tony and Eleanor Carey made a reunion presentation on the Baltimore Careys and its economic, social and philanthropic contributions to the Baltimore area, Maryland, and even beyond. Cecily Hintzen, a Carey/Cary Family member in California, has shared her family research connecting members of the Carey family in Pennsylvania and California. Rex and Janice Carey, Family members in Texas, have shared their research which verifies the connection between the Eastern Shore, Texas and beyond. Peggy and Kenneth Johnston travelled from Texas to attend Carey/Cary Family reunions and share their Cary family research. Also, by coincidence, Helen and Kenneth had previously communicated on-line about their common Simmons heritage (their g-g-g grandfathers), but only through conversation at the reunion did they recognize that they had previously 'connected'! What a surprise...

Ed Carey has gathered and shared extensive information about his Carey Family line which includes Elijah Carey who gave land on which Carey's Church was built. Ed did a presentation of his family research at a Carey/Cary Family reunion. Ed and other family members and friends who have agreed to share their family history research in their chapters of this book are much appreciated.

As indicated earlier, Richard (Rick) Carey's phone message asking about Eastern Shore Careys and his willingness to consider a family reunion were major factors in starting the first Carey family reunion and in the subsequent Carey/Cary Family organization. Rick and Barbara have continued their active and supportive roles in the organization: Rick as president or vice president and Barbara as Communications Director. Barbara's contributions include very attractive and informative folders prepared for reunion participants. Rick's chapter in this book provides additional information about his interest in family history and his leadership in the formation and success of the Carey/Cary Family reunion and organization.

My cousin Barbara Carey Phillips and her husband Bryan have been active and supportive members of the Carey/Cary Family organization from its beginning. When Barbara's sister Margaret Sherkey of FL was unable to continue her role as secretary of the organization, Barbara was elected to that position. In addition to serving in that role, she has been actively involved in reunion programs. On one occasion she enlisted her daughter, Linda Meade, to make a reunion presentation on techniques of gathering, preserving and displaying family artifacts. Later, as indicated previously, Barbara and Dr. Neill Carey made a very entertaining, yet informative reunion presentation on the two Sam Careys from Salisbury. Barbara and Bryan have often helped family members access the Nabb

Center on the Salisbury University campus.

From the time I jokingly suggested that my wife Helen investigate my relationship to Governor Joseph Maull Carey, she has conducted extensive Carey/Cary family research and provided outstanding service and support to the Carey/Cary Family organization. Through her work and creativity in relation to the Carey /Cary Family News, she developed what has proved to be a major communications tool for our research and that of other researchers of Carey/Cary lines. After the organization decided to use a web site for its communication, all existing newsletters were bound and copies were placed in key libraries in the U. S., particularly at institutions with comprehensive family history collections. Over the last twenty-five years, her assorted Carey/Cary files have become thorough and comprehensive. She works tirelessly to support the Carey/ Cary Family.

It should be noted that her chapters in this book provide information about the techniques and resources she has used in researching the Carey/Cary family, as well as her role in editing and publishing the Carey/Cary Family newsletters.

Fortunately, in addition to the service and support of these leaders, the Carey/Cary Family organization has had the consistent and enthusiastic support of several family members. Two come to mind: Jim Joyce and Dorothy Carey. Dorothy has been a consistent attendee at the Carey/Cary reunions. Her late husband, Horace, provided extensive information about his family line, taking Helen and me to the cross roads location identified as Careytown where his parents had a general store. Dorothy and Horace also took us to local cemeteries where family members are interred. Both were always ready to answer our questions of any nature, which has been of great benefit to our research.

Jim Joyce and his late wife, Carol and his sister Ann and her late husband, El Warren, brought a number of family members to an early reunion. From that time, Jim and Ann have been regular reunion attendees. Each year Jim has given a generous donation to the family organization.

Personally, being involved with this family organization has been a positive and rewarding experience. In addition to learning about my own and other Carey/Cary family lines, I have enjoyed the extended family relationships and resulting friendships. Our good friends and family members mentioned here are representative of the Carey/Cary family network that has developed over the last quarter century. Many more family members and their stories will be shared in other chapters of this book.

To celebrate our 61st wedding anniversary, Helen and I will finance publication of this book. We see this as a means of sharing family information with our own family, and to show our appreciation to our relatives and friends who have helped build the Carey/Cary Family organization. We also hope to help others recognize the importance of developing strong and active families in our communities and our society.

SECTION 2

ASSEMBLING AND SHARING CAREY/CARY FAMILY RESEARCH

CHAPTER 4

MY LIFE AND FAMILY HISTORY RESEARCH
- HELEN SIMMONS CAREY -

When would one expect an individual to become interested in researching family history? Since I can only speak for myself, perhaps I should share information about my life before *"family history research."* First, I was born and lived in south Alabama near the Florida panhandle until high school graduation when I left for further education in North Carolina. Four years later and with my parents' encouragement, I moved to Maryland to take a teaching position. Niel and I met as we taught in the same school and married at the end of my first year. We are working on this Carey/Cary project more than sixty years later...

I was fortunate to have had parents who were family-oriented, educated, and focused on providing a good education for my only sibling/older brother and me. However, we had limited contact with other relatives. My mother grew up in Georgia and no members of her family were conveniently located in respect to our home in Opp. My father's siblings moved from Alabama to Louisiana or Texas for further education and later with their spouses. Before I entered school all of my grandparents were deceased with the exception of my maternal grandmother who lived for another twenty years, but never near us. My father had some collateral relatives in Alabama, but my contact with them was limited, leaving vague and few memories. I am more familiar with most of my relatives from my research than first-hand experience.

My purpose in including this personal information is to convey the limited interaction I had with relatives, both direct and collateral. My interest in Carey/Cary family history started with a visit to Cheyenne, WY, and eventually increased as a result of Niel and Rick Carey's plans for a Carey family reunion for sharing family history. Our quest of family history continued as I utilized libraries/facilities in the District of Columbia, Maryland, Delaware, and other states as well as in England, Scotland, Ireland and Wales.[1] Fortunately we have been able to share the information at Carey/Cary family reunions, in our newsletters, and by internet communication.

But let's get on with the story… Let's fast forward about twenty years to 1976 when Niel, our daughters Laura and Rebecca, and I visited Cheyenne, Wyoming, as a part of a three-week auto roundtrip from Maryland to California, using different routes westbound and eastbound.

Our daughters spotted a Carey Street sign in downtown Cheyenne, near the capitol building and its complex of state buildings. In addition to the capitol we visited one of the state¬¬ buildings, believed to have been the Barrett Building, which at that time housed Wyoming's archives and its museum. There we saw a prominent display about Governor Joseph Maull Carey, born in Milton, Delaware (1845-1924).

We quickly learned that Carey Street was named in Governor Carey's honor and that he had headed west after Presi-

1   District of Columbia: Library of Congress, National Archives, DAR Library ; Baltimore, MD: Pratt Library, Maryland Historical Society; Annapolis, MD: Hall of Records, MD State Law Library; Dover DE: DE Public Archives; Salisbury, MD: Nabb Research Center for Delmarva History & Culture; County libraries in Wicomico and Worcester Counties (Salisbury & Snow Hill): and others

dent Ulysses S. Grant (1869-1877) named him the first United States Attorney for the Wyoming Territory. When Wyoming became a state Carey was elected U. S. Senator, eventually its governor and, at one point, Mayor of Cheyenne. Along the way he had become a rancher and is honored in the Cowboy Hall of Fame in Oklahoma City.

Because of the close proximity of Milton, DE, to Niel's childhood home in Maryland, information about the family of Joseph Maull Carey became a point of interest. After our return home we soon visited Milton and its cemeteries, its library, and made the acquaintance of James Tull Carey (Jim) (1912-2000), Milton's Chief of Police. He was friendly and helpful—we learned from him that there were two Carey different family lines in the Milton area—his own and that of the family of Joseph Maull Carey. (*However, in 2019 we learned of a third/separate Carey blood line represented in the Milton area, about which we will provide comment along with the previously identified Carey blood lines, but in my other chapter.*)

Further and as an outgrowth of my developing research we acquired a copy of *Thomas Cary, The Maryland Immigrant*, compiled by Mary Frances Carey of Accomac, VA. The focal point was Thomas Cary who was entered in Maryland records by 1666. Generally it appears that this Thomas Cary family line is thought to be that of many individuals with Carey/Cary heritage from the referenced MD/DE/VA area, referred to as *Delmarva*. Unfortunately it appears that relatively few have confirmed their heritage with DNA samples, according to our current knowledge.

Another publication, *Some of the Carey Family Lines of Sussex County, DE*, compiled by Alfred B. Carey (deceased), outlines descendants of Thomas Carey who either moved to DE or whose location had been affected by the official trans-peninsular MD/DE boundary change in 1769. Personally, my two worn publications are useful but especially because of my hand- written notes in the margins, based on my research or reliable information from others.

However, it is as a result of DNA testing[2] that evidence has been provided that an additional Carey/Cary blood line exists in Delmarva. R. Neill Carey, Samuel W. Carey (one of the sons of the late Charles C. Carey), E. Niel Carey, and Richard G. Carey all have similarity in their DNA. Although unidentified thus far, undoubtedly this second Carey/Cary blood line is more widespread than this group of four Carey/Cary members/friends who chose to participate in our Carey DNA project.

Sam and Neill are both collateral descendants of a Joshua Carey who is "introduced" within the next few paragraphs. On the other hand Niel and Richard (Rick) are second cousins and g-g-g-g-grandsons of a documented common ancestor, Solomon Carey Sr., b. abt 1734. It has been documented that Samuel H. Carey is collaterally related to both R. Neill Carey and Samuel W. Carey and, as a result of DNA testing outcome, Niel and Rick Carey.

Further, to distinguish this DNA-established Carey blood line from that of Thomas Cary, the MD Immigrant, we have searched for a specific ancestor as their reference point. Fortunately we have information provided by the late Samuel H Carey, great-grandson of a Peter Carey. In a 1912 letter

---

2   This DNA testing, the Carey/Cary Project, was sponsored by the Carey/Cary Family organization and conducted through Family Tree DNA. Our member Sean Gilson, who set up our web site, also organized this project. Information about this Carey/Cary DNA Project is available on www.careycary.org. DNA Testing for this project must be through the male Carey/Cary line.

(included below) Samuel H. Carey referenced Joshua Carey (who died in 1850 at age eighty-eight years) as having been his great-grandfather. Additionally, we know from research that Samuel H. Carey is collaterally related to both R. Neill Carey and Samuel W. Carey and, as a result of DNA testing outcome, Niel and Rick Carey as well.

An excerpt from the letter written in 1912 by Samuel H. Carey, Salisbury, MD, in respect to an inquiry from Reverend Joseph Brown Turner is as follows:

"Now since you ask for a report of my branch of the Carey family the same I will give you so far as I learned it from my grandfather (Joshua). When I was about 8 years old. he told me as I recollect that his father Peter Carey came from near Petersburg, Virginia about 1773. He (Joshua) at that time was about 12 years old and his father settled near Whaleyville, Worcester Co., MD he (sic) said he had 2 brothers, Peter & Johnathan (sic). he my grandfather (Joshua) was the youngest. This was about the beginning of the Revolution (sic) War... my grandfather after the death of his first wife married a lady by the name of Bethards for his second wife. They had 5 children, 2 sons and 3 daughters. Oldest son named Henry and youngest Ebenezer. He was my father. He was borned (sic) when my grandfather was sixty years old. my grandfather (Joshua) at that time had moved up to 6 miles of Salisbury, Md. I am now in my 70 years old and a bachler (sic). My grandfather lived to be eighty-eight years old. my brothers and sisters married in this location..."

When Samuel H. Carey, bachelor, died about 1942 he left a detailed will which provided a basis for distribution of his estate. The will not only served his purpose but it provided significant information for researchers. The will distribution included the father of R. Neill Carey (named Samuel S. Carey) and other Carey/Cary Family members. Further, both R. Neill Carey and the late Charles C. Carey (father of Samuel W. Carey) provided information about their own ancestry which is consistent with information derived from the will.

Although E. Niel Carey and Richard G. Carey are not directly descended through the branch outlined by Samuel H Carey, at one time or another their g-g-g-g-grandfather Solomon Carey, Sr., and some descendants, as well as Joshua Carey, lived in the proximity of the Whaleyville/Bishopville (MD) area near present-day MD/DE line. Of interest is that both branches have similarity in name usage. Also in the 1700's Jonathan and Elizabeth (Holloway) Carey lived in that area, including her Holloway family.

From this point we will refer to this second blood line, DNA-based, by the name, *Peter Carey*. As of June 2019 information provided through Family Tree DNA indicates that Peter Carey (b. 1735) is the father of Joshua Carey; later research points to Solomon Carey, Sr., (b. 1734) as having been Peter's brother.

Fortunately, in advance of the final draft of this publication, information was accidentally uncovered as a page-long document from researcher Ruth in Indiana, which must have been in my files for as long as 15-20 years. At the time of its receipt, these contents had no particular meaning, in the absence of a quest to uncover information about Peter Carey. It read:

"Solomon's parents Jonathan Carey (1705-1774) and Elizabeth Carey (1709-1774) . They had four sons, Piercy, Jonathan, Solomon, and Peter. Five daughters Lezia, Kezia, Keren, Mary, Liza." (sic)

In addition, family trees on Ancestry.com have been observed which included the same family configuration as Ruth cited, but unfortunately without specification of sources. However, on page 583 of the 1810 Federal Census, Worcester Co., MD, we located "Solomon Carey of J" as head of household. His survival in 1810 (as son of Jonathan) is consistent with a legal document Solomon Carey signed with his son-in-law Nehemiah Timmons in 1813.

Surprisingly Jonathan and Elizabeth (Holloway) Carey were familiar as a result of my possession of a copy of her will (signed and witnessed by Moses Holloway, Sr., and Aaron Holloway, Jr., 4 Feb. 1774; recorded 6 May 1774. [Worcester Co., MD, Will Book JW4 (1769-83), Folio 226-7] (According to Bessie Holloway's *Holloways of the Eastern Shore* Moses and Aaron were considered 'close family of Elizabeth, perhaps brothers .) In her will Elizabeth named "my daughter Piercy Hamlin", "my son Solomon Cary", "my daughter Hezia (sic) Ridley", "daughter Kerenhappuch Shockley", and "my daughter Mary Cary" as Exectrix.

The discrepancy in the children's names provided by Ruth in Indiana include Piercy (shown as a son); Lezia (instead of Hezia) and Lisa, all named as daughters; and exclusion of the sons Jonathan and Peter. Also and significantly, the absence of the names of sons Jonathan Cary and Peter Cary in the will can be attributed to the death of either or both sons prior to her death in 1774.

In support of the family relationship between Solomon Carey and sister Piercy (Hamlin) Worcester Land Records include an item indicating *Carey's Chance*, 50 acres of land patented for Solomon Carey in 1760 in West Berlin district #9 map 27, was sold in 1761 to George Hamblin, Piercy's husband.

Joshua Carey, aforementioned as son of Peter Carey, was born about 1764. In turn, this suggests that Peter (born 1736) appears to have died between 1764 and 1774—before Elizabeth's will was written. As for Jonathan (born 1731), the father's name *Jonathan* would have had priority in respect to the naming of sons. Consequently it is likely that one of the sons had been given that name and , further, that Jonathan was one of their children although not named in Elizabeth Carey's 1774 will, possibly because of his death as well.

Family tradition is that Elizabeth H. Carey's husband, Jonathan, who was born about 1705, died about 1772. Unfortunately the date of his demise remains undocumented. We do know that Jonathan Carey was shown on a judicial record of (then) Somerset County two times in 1738. In 1755 Jonathan Carey, Planter, again appeared on a Somerset Judicial Record, but as a Surety.

In addition we have a copy of a Land Warrant, Certificate of Survey, and Patent for Worcester County, MD, land surveyed for and patented to Jonathan Carey. *Jonathan's Choice* was show as "Ex'd and passed, 17th Oct. 1764".

This recorded information provides support for Jonathan Carey having survived at least within ten years of his projected date of death. Perhaps further information will be uncovered. If he had no property at the time of his death he would not necessarily have been required to have a will. However, it would seem that, according to practice, there would have been documents associated with his death intestate.

However, it should be noted that in the 1700's, as well as

1800's, records in courthouses, churches, and homes were subject to fires. The paper on which records were written was apt to deteriorate and ink fades. Many individuals did not read, write, and/or cipher, minimizing the personal records which were kept, such as Bible records.

Further, Solomon Carey Sr.'s children were Solomon, Jr., Jonathan, Saul Grindy and Catherine (Catty) (married Nehemiah Timmons). In particular Jonathan and Solomon have frequently been used as names in this Carey blood line, both for ancestors and descendants in Maryland and Delaware, as well as by those migrating west, particularly Indiana and states in that vicinity.

It should be noted that, by comparison with records after 1850 , the nature and availability of legal records before 1850 lessens, but even more so during the 1700's and prior years. It seems appropriate to adapt research expectations accordingly. Consequently, in my opinion, the outcome that Jonathan and Elizabeth Carey are the common ancestors for Niel /Rick and Neill/Sam has adequate documentation support, considering the limit of the records in this time period. Research of this nature is generally on-going and may be strengthened by 'newly appearing ' records. However, we cannot ignore the fact that any conclusion might be disputed by later documentation.

Thus, moving on, over the years I have sought documented information about the link of Thomas Cary, the Maryland Immigrant, to his heritage, which would have been prior to coming to the New World. In her *Thomas Cary of Monye Creek and Worcester County, MD, Descendants* Mary Frances Carey wrote that "…There is little doubt that Thomas Cary of Monye Creek, born 1610-1620, was a descendant of the Carys of England, and a probable member of the sixteenth or seventeenth generation. Just how he connects to the line is not clear."

On the other hand Alfred B. Carey, in his *Some of the Carey Lines Who Descended From Thomas Cary, The Immigrant, and The English Pedigree*, specified that "there was little doubt" that Thomas was a nephew of James Cary (who settled in Charlestown, MA, in 1639). He further indicated that James (1600-1681) was son of William, Mayor of Bristol in 1611. He also cited John as a brother of James Cary, that John "did not emigrate to America…", but "Thomas Cary (b. 1613) was a son of John (1583-1661)…" Relevant comments of Alfred B. Carey can be located in his monograph on pp. 10-15, although, from my perspective, he provides secondary information instead of primary needed for actual documentation.

However, of even more significance in respect to what Alfred Carey provides as ancestry of Thomas Cary (who first appeared in Maryland colony records in 1666) is located in his monograph on page 23, Chapter III, Thomas Cary, The Immigrant, Sixteenth Generation. He indicated as follows: "Thomas Cary, b. 1613 – will made 1681, probated 1686 in Maryland, son of John Cary, 1583-1666." Further, he wrote that Thomas was married twice, first to Susanna Limberry of Devon and then to Jane.

It should be noted that, because of the records' lack of documented information about Thomas Cary's ancestry, Niel and I traveled to England in spring 1998 with Thomas Cary's ancestry as our focus for the entire two weeks. His heritage had, however, already been a strong interest on previous trips in spring 1994 and fall 1995, and particularly the latter.

In addition, although info will be included about all three trips, it seems appropriate to first interject a reference to "Thomas Cary Mystery Continued" by David Carey, from the newsletter of Summer 1999, Volume 4, Issue 2, pp.1,10, available on www.careycary.org .

In his article David Carey, now deceased, wrote:

"...Thomas Cary, the London Merchant, had a son John who was quite active and renowned in the Virginia Colony and in English politics and commerce. John and two of his cousins sent pedigrees to the Royal College of Heralds to obtain permission to use the Cary nobles'coat of arms. Niel and Helen (Carey) found a copy of John's own pedigree in the Society of Genealogists in London. It included notes, possibly by the College of Heralds investigator as follows: 1671 15/12 Admon. To John Cary son of Susan Cary widow – p. St. Saviorellico in Jewry-London." ("Admon." is an abbreviation for admonishment, an archaic term for instructions to the administrators of an estate.)"

"The pedigree itself identified John's parents as Thomas and Susan Carey, while the notes provide proof that his father, Thomas Cary, of London, died before 1671. Thomas Cary, the MD Immigrant, continued to appear in MD records until his will was probated on 17 June 1687. So the two Thomas Carys could not have been one and the same person. Niel and Helen's discovery completes the vital record of Thomas Cary, the London Merchant, and disproves Alfred B. Carey's claim that he was also the MD Immigrant. The ancestry of Thomas Cary, the MD Immigrant, remains a mystery."

Further, detail about our Thomas Cary research in England in 1998 appears in two later newsletter issues: Volume 6, Issue 1, Winter/Spring 2001 and Volume 7, Issue 1, Winter/Spring 2002. *"Researching Car(e)ys in England, Part I"* is located in 2001 issue and its Part II, in 2002, both on page 1. (All issues are available on www.careycary.org .)

Additional related articles are in the same 2001 and 2002 issues: *"Madm Carey's Will"*, p. 4, *"Putney Parish Church and Mary Cary's Memorial"*, p. 5, in 2001 and *"Putney Parish Church and Roehampton House"* , p.5 in 2002. These several articles in 2001 and 2002 issues integrate with the detailed information found in Parts I and II, referenced in the previous paragraph. It should be noted that the Thomas Cary cited could not have been the same as Thomas Carey, The MD Immigrant.

In retrospect, our 1998 itinerary had included a full week in London and a second week in the vicinity of Bristol. During our first week we located in the Wimbledon area, southwest London and near Public Records Office (PRO) [England's national archives in Kew (district in London borough Richmond)]. We were also able to use the London subway system to access the Family Research Center, the British Library, Library of the Society of Genealogists, and that at Lambeth Palace. Following our usual practice of dividing the work according to our interests and talent, generally Niel focused on the broader historical picture while I worked on the family genealogy.

With the availability of our rental car as needed, we were able to visit several places of special significance for Carey/Cary researchers. The Lord Hunsdon (Henry Carey) memorial in Westminster Abbey (the tallest and, in our opinion, the most magnificent monument in the abbey); the (1691) site of

John Cary's office on Botolph Lane; and Roehampton House, the beautiful country home that Thomas Cary (son of John) built west of London in Putney—supposedly to escape the dust, smells, and diseases of 18th century London.

After we left London we stayed at a charming B&B, hosted by Margaret and 'Fen' in the village of Calne in Wiltshire. Since we were so pleased with their B&B, we modified our original plans and 'commuted' to and from Bristol. The drive to the Bristol Records Office (BRO), with its traffic and confusing street configuration, was a reminder of our previous experience in 1995. Fortunately, just as we experienced in London, the BRO staff was knowledgeable and helpful. We also visited churches and as well as sites of former churches mentioned in Car(e)y family history. Although we gathered much information in Bristol, it did not seem to be directly related to Thomas Cary, the MD Immigrant—believed by many to have departed Bristol for the New World. However, over time the information has been useful in other ways.

Finally, since Calne is on the southern edge of the Cotswolds, we took advantage of the short period of sunny weather to visit this charming and quaint part of England as we returned to a London airport to return to the United States.

In addition, it seems that we should mention our trip to southwest England in spring 1994, visiting places that Niel had frequented during his earlier stay of three years as a member of the U.S. Air Force in the 1950's, while stationed at the former English Army hospital at Guy's Marsh, near Shaftesbury, Dorset. We visited Bath, Castle Cary, Cardiff, Salisbury, Torquay, and Bournemouth. Even though we spent three days in Cockington Village near Torre Abbey, we did not have time to research the Carey/Cary family there or in Bristol. Sadly our itinerary was cut short near its end when we were notified that my 99-year old father had died in Alabama.

Further, in October 1995 Niel and I once again traveled to England, this time with the primary object of gathering information about the Carey/Cary family and visiting places with family connections. We landed at Gatwick Airport, picked up a rental car and drove to Chartwell, Churchill's home. Because Sir George Carey was the Archbishop of Canterbury we decided to visit that city and see its magnificent cathedral before we reversed direction and traveled to southwest England, which includes counties of Devon, Somerset, and Dorset.

On the way to southwest England we stopped to see Bob Cary,[3] who lives in the Village or Steyning and who had corresponded with Rick and me. He invited us to his home and to meet his family members, Joy and his mother, who were great hosts and shared Carey family pictures and info. They gave us a tour of their village and of the resort city of Brighton.

Our first major destination was the city of Torquay, which includes the restored village of Cockington. We spent three days in this area, visiting Torre Abbey and the Manor House and church in Cockington Village. Several members of the Cary family lived in this area from the 1500s to the 1800s. Members of the family represented the area in the English parliament, they served several English monarchs in various roles and responsibilities, they were leaders in the Church, and they were actively involved in military activities, including the defense of the region against the Spanish Armada.

From the Torquay area we went west to Clovelly, which is

---

[3]   www.careycary.org , see newsletter Volume 4, Issue 2, 1999, p. 1, article "Clarence Cary, 'Boy Hero'". Bob Cary forwarded a photocopy of a card, asking for info about Midshipman Cary, described as one of America's Heroes 1864, etc., and about Ft. Fisher. Bob's message led to a heavily researched article about Clarence & renown family.

also in Devon and which flourished under Cary family leadership during the 1600's and 1700's. We were interested in visiting this quaint village, which has only one narrow street which descends deeply to a harbor and the shores of the Bristol Channel. The street is so steep and narrow that it can be traveled only by foot or on the back of the famous Clovelly donkeys.[4] We also visited the nearby Parish Church All Saints with its fine monuments dating back to the 18th Century.

Next came a visit to Bristol where we were able to obtain a considerable amount of information about the Carey/Cary family, which we are still analyzing. However, we were able to determine that members of the Carey/Cary family were actively involved in the governance of that city and in shipping, as well as aspects of a growing interest in the "colonies" of America. Incidentally, we also found references which confirmed our notion that the Cary/Carey spellings are interchangeable.

After we left Bristol we visited the village of Castle Cary. Ancient records indicate that Adam de Cary lived at the castle but today all that remains of the castle is a mound in the middle of beautiful, pastoral English countryside. The stately and impressive ruins of Glastonbury Abbey, an important place in the legend of King Arthur, are nearby.

Our visit gave me a much stronger feeling of kinship across the ages, with our ancestors. Moreover, I could easily understand how Henry Grosvenor Cary, author of *The Cary Family in England*, was able to state "The Cary family in England is

---

4   Response1995 to *Carey Family* from John Rous, Clovelly Estate Co., LTD, Clovelly, Devon. Thanks for letter 23 Mar. & regret that documentation of Cary family history associated with Clovelly was destroyed in major fires of Manor House Clovelly Court in 1789,1943. We believe Cary family's male line at Clovelly ended in late 17th C. Estate including Manor House was sold to Zachary Hamlyn in 1738; successors to his family have owned Manor ever since. (Rous, collateral descendant.) Also, research may occur at public records office at Barnstaple in Devon.

one of the oldest, as it has been one of the most illustrious and honored in the kingdom."[5]

Further, although perhaps considered unique, both in 2003 and 2004 Niel and I took advantage of Caribbean ports by leaving our cruise ship in Barbados to visit its library. "We knew from prior research that at least as early as the 1600's it was not uncommon for immigrants from England to have Barbados as their destination or to stop off en route to the 'west'. Some stayed in the Caribbean while others resumed travel at a later time. We sought an answer: Is there any possibility that Thomas Cary went through customs in Barbardos?

Once we knew that our cruise was to stop in Barbados, we utilized the Internet to gather information about its library with genealogical records... Although the library's holdings were modest at best, it did have a collection of *The Journal of the Barbados Museum and Historical Society* in bound form. Our intent was to gather as much information as our couple of hours would permit, without otherwise researching any particular Car(e)y. We each had our own paper and pencil and functioned as if we were in a marathon."[6] Our transcribed items were published in the newsletter, as noted in the footnote — *unfortunately without Thomas...*

On our next cruise to the area in 2004 we repeated the process with another visit to the same library in Bridgetown, St. Michael, Barbados. The additional transcribed items were placed in the *Carey/Cary Family News, Volume 12, Issue 1, Spring/Summer 2007*, p. 6. Although we never had feedback from researchers who benefited from the information, we thought it had potential as a resource and enjoyed our library project!

---

5   Compiled by Niel Carey, 1996
6   Carey/Cary Family News, Volume 8, Issue 1, Spring 2003, p. 4. www.careycary.org

Finally, because of an unconfirmed indication that Thomas Cary, the MD Immigrant, was born in 1633 in Ross and Comarty County, Scotland, in 2006 Niel and I took advantage of an opportunity to 'experience' Scotland and also visit research facilities in search of info about his possible birth there. In Edinburgh we visited the General Register Office for Scotland where the index for the Church of England Old Parish Registers (OPR), Births and Baptisms were checked for Thomas Cary, but he was not listed. Records at the time of his birth were spotty and, even now, Ross and Cromarty area remains desolate.

We also visited the Edinburgh Room, Edinburgh Central Library, George IV Bridge, Edinburgh, but had no success in locating records related to Thomas Cary at the appropriate time/location.

Although we were unable to determine if Thomas Cary was actually born in Scotland, we did leave with several items which should be included in consideration for further research on this topic. One is to identify a substantive basis for a family tradition that he was born in Scotland. Another is conjecture that *clearances* might *not* have been a factor in relation to his conjectured emigration from Scotland to the colonies. Later we learned that the *clearances* apparently occurred at least a century after Thomas Cary appeared in MD records in 1666.

Although we were unable to determine that Thomas Cary was born in Scotland, we benefitted from an educational experience in respect to research in Scotland. Also we became aware of www.scotlandspeople.gov.uk , which is a partnership between the General Register Office for Scotland, the National Archives of Scotland and the Court of the Lord Lyon, ... enabled by Scotland-on-Line, a leading provider of web based business solutions.

In conclusion, during the last twenty-five years or more our Carey/Cary Family research has been interesting, productive and challenging. We have learned a great deal about Carey/Cary Family lines, but further research may increase our knowledge, provide responses to unanswered questions, and lead to the creation of new questions.

JOIN IN...

- Helen Simmons Carey

B.A. from Duke University, M.Ed. from University of Maryland College Park; Mathematics Teacher, Baltimore County, MD: 1957-1963; School Counselor, Baltimore County, MD: junior high 1963-1983, high school 1983-1993; Ruling Elder, Mt. Hebron Presbyterian Church, Ellicott City, MD, 1983-1986; President, The Legends at Turf Valley Homeowners' Assn.: 2001-2004, 2013-2016; Editor, *Carey/Cary Family News*, 1994-2009; Member, Daughters of the American Revolution (DAR)

CHAPTER 5

MY SEARCH FOR CAREY ANCESTORS
IN SUSSEX COUNTY, DELAWARE AND BEYOND
- DIANE HANSEN -

My search for my family history began at my mother's dining room table in the early 1970s. In my mid-twenties at that time, I hadn't given much thought to my forebears. But when my mother's after-dinner narrative turned to family history, both hers and my father's, I soon found paper and pencil and began recording. Later I wished that I had started recording sooner! By the time we finally got up to clear the table, the one yellow page of scribbling covered both sides and the margins. It was in no order; it mixed stories from both sides of the family together. It would be almost 10 years before I seriously tried to decipher these writings and learn more about these unknown people, my ancestors.

Of my four family lines, I chose to search for my Carey ancestry first because I (foolishly) thought it would be easier! After all, our Carey records would be in the English language; no need to learn German, Polish or Russian. And the records would be here in the USA, just a short drive away! As you can see, I was quite delusional when I started this search.

Personal computers, the internet, the world-wide-web weren't in use when I began but I soon learned that the Ft.Worth (TX) library had a very large genealogy department. You could find me there almost every Saturday. I hadn't yet learned enough about researching to consider having an organized plan, or objectives, or goals and even some discipline (the discipline still eludes me today). If it said CAREY, CARRY, CARY, KERRY, KERI, etc., I wrote it down or copied it! The making of large and still larger stacks of copies made me feel, at the time, that I was making great progress in locating my family! Silly me!

Today, almost 50 years later, I'm still searching! And I'm still surrounded by stacks of paper. But now my head is awash with Carey names, dates, facts, figures, map locations, and dozens of cemetery names and locations.

However, it's probably safe for me to say that despite my best efforts I will never find my roots tracing back to Charlemagne, King Richard III or Genghis Khan, like some of Henry Gates guests do. I'm still hoping that someday I may find the name of my 4th Great-grandfather, Mr. Unknown Carey, from Sussex County Delaware.

So what were some of my stumbling blocks? Why am I still wallowing around in all things Carey?

Original, first-person records created by my Delaware ancestors in the 1800s don't appear to exist. My early ancestors did not read or write. So there weren't any brittle, faded letters in any of our family attics, either in Delaware or in Indiana. Nor were there any cherished family Bibles, or diaries, in which they would have recorded their special events or daily activities. My ancestor, g-g-grandfather William Carey, who moved his family to Indiana in 1869, could not read or write, except for being able to sign his name.

Fortunately, a brief letter written in 1930 to my great-grandfather, Harvey Carey, survived over the years. The author, Harvey's cousin, William H. Workman, wrote about Brownsville, TX, where he and his wife lived, heading up that location of the Volunteers of America. He described the wonderful lush, fertile Rio Grande valleys where migrant workers harvested all types of fruit and produce. He also reminisced about the big move in 1869 that took some of our family far away from Delaware to Starke County, Indiana.

A few years ago, I located a surviving descendant of William H. Workman and was able to provide him with a copy of his ancestor's wonderful letter. He was thrilled to receive the copy and told me that he couldn't wait to share it with his elderly mother! The original of that letter is now, I believe, with a cousin's family and I hope they cherish it as much as I appreciate the copy of it that they shared with me.

The scribbled 1970's notes have survived also, and with much thanks to the excellent recall and memories of my mother and other family members, I have been able to create a brief outline of our Carey family from Delaware.

MY CIRCUMSTANTIAL FAMILY TREE

I often tell people that I have a "circumstantial" family tree. It's circumstantial because many of those critical pieces of hard evidence, the "smoking guns" (documents, letters, Bibles, etc.) just aren't to be found. In their absence, I've spent a great deal of my research time determining which people or lineages are NOT mine. Through this process of elimination, I've traced the story of much of our Carey lineage coming forward from ancestor Stephen Carey's birth in Delaware in the early 1800s.

PEOPLE MAKE MISTAKES - HURRAY!

People make mistakes; nothing new about that. We don't

usually applaud mistakes but sometimes a mistake works in one's favor. One such mistake, made more than 100 ago yet ultimately created a wonderful document describing my Carey family--and it is in William Carey's own words! To date, it is the only source document that I have which contains this much family data.

After our reunited government finally recovered sufficiently from our country's greatest conflict, the War of the Rebellion, better known as the Civil War, our historians, archivists and librarians began to collect, store and record the vast amounts of data detailing the history and the human toil of this war. While this massive project was on-going, one anonymous worker made an innocent mistake about William H. Carey's service to his country. This mistake, however, wasn't discovered until 1913, when my William H. Carey retired and decided to apply for Civil War pension. He sought out a local attorney who took his information and wrote to Washington to obtain a copy of William's service record during the Civil War. When the folder arrived, the attorney queried William as to whether this was his record and William said to the effect "If it says William Carey on it, it must be mine." So the attorney mailed off his application.

A short while later, the fireworks began! Uncle Sam was very angry! The message sent back to his attorney was that this man applying for Civil War pension was an Imposter! The real William Carey was alive and well in Delaware and already collecting his pension.

What a difference one little middle initial can make! My William H. Carey, as I said earlier, could not read or write, so he assumed they had sent the correct file. After all, it was the correct company and regiment in which he served. The angry attorney asked him why he was claiming to be William P. Carey. My g-g-grandfather denied that, and told the attorney that he was William H. Carey, but he couldn't read or write, just his name was all. The attorney was surprised to learn this as William H. Carey was a respected member of his community, a member of the town council, so everyone just assumed that he was literate.

William went on to tell the attorney that there were four Careys in Delaware's 6th Regiment, Co. K: William P. Carey, William H. Carey, and their brothers, respectively, George Carey and Robert Carey. Two other family members also served with them--Elizabeth Carey's husband, James Purnel Workman and Eunice Carey's husband, John Boughton/ Bowden.

When this information was conveyed to Washington, they appointed a Special Examiner to look into the matter. This investigation took the Examiner, and William also, back to Delaware to locate and question the surviving members of this regiment almost 50 years after the war's end! The conclusion by the Special Examiner was that there were indeed two William Careys serving in that particular company and regiment but only one folder, under the name of William P. Carey, was originally created to hold these records. A new record was created for our William H. Carey, the data separated and corrected, and William H. Carey was added to the Civil War history files for the state of Delaware.

But did he get his pension, you ask? No! To obtain pension, the soldier had to have 90 days or more of PAID service time during the war. My William's total paid service time did not meet these requirements. Our government often had difficulties meeting its financial obligations during the war and many of the home-guard members, who were activated spo-radically, did not receive all the monies they were due, and subsequently were not eligible to receive a pension. But long after the fact, and despite being denied a pension, I'm sure that William was happy to have his war record corrected and his service recognized.

So how did this mistake help me out 100 years later? William had to answer all the same questions for the Special Examiner that all the other old soldiers did. And in his multi-page typed deposition, William named his parents (including his mother's maiden name) and the names of each of his siblings! God bless those mistake makers!

But that wasn't all that it provided. One respondent confirmed his recollection of the two Williams by noting that he knew William H. Carey's father, Stephen Carey, and that he was a fine man. Corroboration - excellent! Another aging soldier remembered William because he recalled that William's sister Nicey (Eunice) married one of the Boughton (Bowden) boys. Yes, more corroboration!

Of course, however, I'd be remiss if I omitted the comments of another old soldier who remembered William P. Carey, the carpenter, with an excellent knowledge of English and mathematics, so smart that they chose him as their sergeant. Of course, the old soldier remembered the other William, too - William H. Carey, describing him as the young, dumb one! Yes - that is my ancestor!

By examining both service and pension files, I was also able to learn additional information about his eldest brother, Robert. After Robert died in 1892, his wife Clarissa (nee Long) applied to continue to receive his pension payments. Her testimony was supported by Gumborough/Gumboro residents Philip and Mary E. (nee West) Carey who noted they had known both Robert and Clarissa all their lives. (*Notes: 1. I'm still trying to determine if this Philip Carey is also connected in some way to our Carey line. 2. There is a very complete Long Family History document in the Genealogy room of the Snow Hill Library in Worcester County, Maryland that includes Clarissa Long's ancestry.*)

That trip to the National Archives produced vital information about my family tree. I hope someday to make a repeat visit and review records of other collateral relatives whose names I've since discovered. I'm sure there are many more nuggets of information in those files there that could help round out our Carey family tree. (*Note: My research at the Archives was done in the 1990s and some of their information may be available now on-line.*)

On another trip, a business associate, also into genealogy, contacted a relative who was completing a research project for the National Genealogy Association, headquartered at that time in an old historic home and carriage house in Virginia. We took the Metro to its last stop and were met by his cousin who allowed us to browse the stacks of the Association's library for a few hours that evening while she worked on her project. It was here that I found a book entitled Churches of Sussex County Delaware, which detailed the churches'excerpts from the 1868 maps of the Delaware Hundreds. One map showing the area around Gumboro contained locations and names of land owners and I soon found what appeared to be my g-g-grandfather's home, and also the home of his brother, Thomas. Item "Visit GumborolGumborough" was added to my genealogy To-Do list. That item, however, had to wait until the next Washington visit which did not occur until February 2001. (*Note: Copies of the 1868 maps of all the Hundreds in Sussex County are available for purchase at the Dover Archives in Dover DE.*

These maps are excellent for providing landowner names and identify-
ing early roads that existed in 1868.)

My ancestor Stephen Carey was born between 1800-1810
according to the Federal Census Records. His marriage bond
dated 21 June 1829 states he was from Broad Kiln (Kill) Hundred and his bride, Sophia Timmons, was from Broad Creek
Hundred. Their first child, a son named Robert, was born 2
October 1829. In the following years, four more sons and 3
daughters followed (not listed in any specific order): James,
Thomas, William, Woolsey, Eunice, Elizabeth and Nancy. Oral
history says Sophia died shortly after her last child, Woolsey,
was born in 1842 or 1843.

Some mystery still surrounds the parents of Sophia Timmons but available records seem to suggest Sophia was one of
the nine children born to Ezekiel Timmons and Eunice Morris.
Eunice/Unice was the daughter of Robert and Polly Morris. In
his will, proved on 9 January 1818, Robert left items to his
granddaughter Mary Ann Johnson and grandson Robert Timmons, $25 to his wife Polly, and the remainder of his estate to
his daughter Nicey (Eunice) married to Ezekiel Timmons the
Younger. He also appointed Ezekiel Timmons as his executor.

Other research indicates Mary Ann Johnson is probably
the wife of Ananias Johnson, the same Ananias who put up
the $200 marriage bond for Ezekiel Timmons in 1850. And
Mary Ann's brother, Robert Timmons, appears to have taken
his inherited horse and saddle and joined the migration of people moving west.

The 1830 Federal Census shows the household of Stephen
Carey including an elderly female who was biologically too old
to be Stephen's or Sophia's parent. I believe this to be Sophia's
grandmother, Polly Morris, widow of Robert Morris (d.1818)

and I believe Stephen and Sophia took up residency with Sophie's Grandma Polly soon after they married. They needed a home quickly since first child Robert's birth was rapidly approaching! This same elderly woman is living with them according to the 1840 census, as well.

Ezekiel Timmons (identified as Ezekiel the Younger on early land deeds) died 7 July 1847. In 1848, his widow, Unice/Eunice, filed a petition in Orphans Court to have her widow's dower restored to her. In this document she states that she and Ezekiel were married 1 March 1792. Of their nine children, five were still living at the time she filed her petition. She states that the Sheriff seized her and Ezekiel's lands for unpaid debts in 1830 and the land was sold at Public Sale in March 1830. She requested that one third of the lands, tenements and hereditaments be restored to her during her natural life. There is no evidence, however, in the folder at the Dover Archives to indicate whether any action was ever taken on Unice/Eunice's request. Furthermore, neither Unice/Eunice Timmons or her mother, Polly Morris, appear in the 1850 census, leading one to assume that one or both may have died by that time.

Delaware Land records in 1847 show that Stephen Carey purchased land near Pear Tree Road and Lowe's Crossing Road from John and Jane Morris. About this same time Burton West also purchased land, abutting Stephen's property, from John and Jane Morris. One of the boundaries listed for Stephen's land was the "old steam mill road", which was located about one-quarter mile south of today's intersection of Lowe's Crossing Road and Pear Tree Road. This steam mill road ran east from Pear Tree Road and connected to the Gumboro/Millsboro Road. In more recent times the old steam mill road had been renamed Short's Road, per the road marker, until the unused road was obliterated sometime around 2009. (Note: At one time, all the land south of the old steam mill road was owned by various Short families, hence the name change to Short's Road.)

About 1855 Burton West is selling his land to I. Short, and stated it included lands he had purchased from Stephen Carey. I have not, however, found a record for the sale of Stephen's land to West, or evidence that this land may have passed along to his heirs. Perhaps research will tell.

OTHER KNOWN DATA ABOUT
STEPHEN AND SOPHIA'S CHILDREN

Robert Carey, b. 1829, married Clarissa Long (daughter of David Long and Nancy Lewis) 23 March 1857, from Selbyville. They raised their family in Bishopville MD just south of Selbyville, DE. Robert, Clarissa and their eldest son, David, are buried in the Selbyville Cemetery. Other family members are buried at the Bishopville Oddfellows Cemetery. Their children were: David H. (Frances) Carey, Julia E. (Edward Irving Elliott), Anna, Lenora (Gillis Walker); and James Thomas Carey (Susan).

James Carey - Named by William as a brother but I have found no information about James.

Elizabeth Carey married James Purnel Workman 22 Apr. 1849; had children Sophia, William H., Amelia J., John T., and Theo. I have found no other lineal descendents from Purnal and Elizabeth except through William H. Workman, who wrote the 1930 letter. My correspondence with his descendant, "Buddy" Hanna, stated he had found no other surviving lineages either. Elizabeth and her husband stayed only two years in Delphi, Carroll County, Indiana, and they returned to Delaware. I do not know why they moved back.

Thomas Carey married Ester/Hester Short, and they are buried in the back row of the Odd Fellows cemetery on Iron Branch Road in Dagsboro. Buried next to them are Mary and Philip Short, Hester's parents. (Note: Inscriptions are on the back side of the stones.) Surviving children were George W. Carey, b.1870, and Oscar 1. b. 1873. Two other children, noted in census records, apparently did not survive to adulthood.

Eunice Jane Carey married John Wesley Bowden and their family moved to Panola County, MS. Children were Sophia, Julia Caroline, and Isaac.

Nancy L. Carey married Seth Baker 9 Dec. 1858. Children --= Eliza J., Sarah L., Ella L., Mary C., Archa S., Thomas G., Cora D., Lillie A., Isaac A. Other researchers say that Nancy died about 1880 but I have not found a record yet to confirm this.

William Henry Harrison Carey married 1) Mary A. Davis, and had children Thomas, Harvey F., Lorenzo, Anna, Sarah Jane (sometimes listed as Jane Sarah), William H., Jr., Mary D., and Everett Merl. After Mary's death, William married 2) Augusta Rossow, a widow. William Carey and both of his wives are buried in Hobart IN Cemetery.

There were work opportunities in Starke County as both William and Woolsey found jobs with the railroads that criss-crossed the county. William and his family remained in Starke County almost 10 ° years before moving to a small Porter County town named Wheeler, IN, and rented a place to live. William later bought a farm nearby and farmed for many years before retiring to Hobart, Indiana.

Woolsey Carey, the youngest child of Stephen and Sophia, was born in 1842 or 1843. Woolsey was raised by, or lived with, his elder sister, Elizabeth Workman. Woolsey attempted to enlist with other family members in Delaware units formed during the Civil War, but he was rejected because of an unspecified handicap. I don't know whether Woolsey returned to Delaware with sister Elizabeth's family or continued to stay with William and his family in Oregon Twp., Starke County, IN, and work for the railroad. No other info about Woolsey has been found.

WHY INDIANA?

The questions I pondered for many years were why did William and others in his family make the decision to move west? Was Starke County, IN, a specific destination for them or did they just decide that it looked like a good place to stop and make a new home?

Information from another Timmons descendent and researcher, the late Mary Coovert, shared with me by Helen Carey, may provide the simple answers: word of mouth and letters home.

Apparently the early settlers gave very good press to Indiana's lands. Coovert's well- documented research about her Matthias Timmons family indicates Timmons descendents with surnames of Timmons, Jarman, German and Prettyman moved west and lived and died in various Indiana counties, among them White, Carroll, Kosciusko and Starke Counties. Others settled in Indiana only to move again when more frontier lands were cleared of Indians and the Indian lands became available for settlement in Iowa and Nebraska.

MORE FAMILY?

When I studied the 1870, 1880 and 1900 censuses, I learned quite a bit more about William Carey's family. There were more children than I ever heard discussed by anyone in our family. The boys, Harvey, Thomas and Lorenzo, and their families, were frequently mentioned and sometimes found in old photos. But the census indicated there were other children, too. What happened to them?

The first Indiana census to capture our family's information in Indiana was 1870. William and Mary had a daughter named Annie, born in Delaware, who made the long trek with her family to their new home.

But by 1880 she was no longer with them. Unfortunately, most of the counties were not yet recording birth and death information routinely. I assume she passed away from Injury or illness as many young children did, and she may be buried in an unknown grave in Starke County, IN.

Daughter Mary apparently did not survive childhood. I have found no death record or place of burial for her. There were several Lake County marriage records for Mary Careys, but most were people from outside the state of Indiana. At that time Lake County had very few requirements for people getting married, so it had a reputation as a quick "marriage mill" destination and people often come from surrounding states to get married in Indiana.

Son William H. Carey, Jr. died in 1900 at age 24. As a child he suffered a severe head injury that produced paralysis and later strokes. In February 1903, William's wife, Mary A. (nee Davis), died of paralysis after a prolonged illness. In 1905 daughter Sarah Jane, 31 years old, died after suffering from epilepsy since childhood. She had given birth to a son, Lynne, the previous year. Lynne died as a teen-ager. All four of these family members are buried in the Hobart Cemetery, in Hobart IN.

With three family members suffering from serious illnesses that required almost constant care, a neighboring widow, with a family of her own to support, worked for William Carey taking care of his family members and doing housekeeping for them. Her name was Augusta Rossow. In April 1903, after Mary's death, Augusta became the new Mrs. William Carey.

William's youngest son, Everett Merl, was almost missed in my early research. He was born in the mid-1880s and the 1890 census, which would have recorded his arrival into the family, burned. He appeared briefly in the 1900 census and then he seemed to disappear, much like Annie and Mary. If Everett's name had not appeared in his father's obituary notice in 1916, I might have presumed that he was another child that William and Mary had lost to illness or injury. In 1916, Everett, his wife Gusta, and their family were living in New Philadelphia, IN. I didn't locate Everett again until the release of the 1930 census which showed that he and his family had moved to Corpus Christi, TX.

Over the years, as more documents became available on the web, additional information emerged about Everett's life. Apparently he left home when he was in his teens, and he and girlfriend, Tracy Ashton, several years older than he, were married in Chicago. They lived in Michigan, with at least one daughter, and at some point they parted ways. Tracy died young and her two daughters were raised in Indiana by her parents.

DEJA VU!

You don't have to be clairvoyant, psychic, or have extrasensory abilities of any type to find your ancestors, but I've found that my body and mind occasionally seem to sense more about my surroundings than I consciously realize. For example, one raw, wet and windy Monday while cousin Jan and I were getting acquainted with the Indian River area of Delaware, we located another cemetery in Dagsboro that we hadn't visited yet.

Gulf storms had progressed up the eastern American coastline the week of the Carey/Cary Reunion and the harsh weather conditions were not conducive for our usual Monday, post-reunion, cemetery walks. Until we found this cemetery, we had been content that day to simply tour by auto. I entered the horseshoe-shaped drive, and with my handy spotter glasses, tried to read as many inscriptions as possible despite the heavy rain and high winds. After the first pass, I turned the car around and drove thru the cemetery the opposite way to pick up any other names we might have missed. Just pass the halfway point of the horseshoe arch, I stopped the car and told Jan to look at the hair on my arms and neck--it suddenly was standing straight up! I recognized the feeling instantly and said "Jan, there are Careys in this cemetery!"

She watched with some dismay as I grabbed an umbrella, a pen and a tablet and went out into the raging elements. I walked straight to the back of the cemetery which seemed to be where I was supposed to go. My hopes dashed, however, when I noticed many stones appeared to be without inscriptions. Worn away, I thought! Undaunted, I walked to the back side of the row and there they were -- inscriptions on the older graves were facing the back of the cemetery. Four separate stones in the row - Thomas Carey, Ester Carey, Mary Short and Phillip Short. Ester's stone tied it together very succinctly -- "wife of Thomas Carey, daughter of Phillip and Mary Short." I like it when they tell me their history and I don't have to look it up!

After checking Find-A-Grave when I got home, I learned that Robert Carey's daughter Lenora, and her husband, Gillie/ Gideon Walker, are also buried at this cemetery. Their only daughter, Edith, married Dr. Dodds from Dagsboro and they had an adopted daughter. After Dr. Dodds' rather early death, Edith married Gideon Littleton in Millsboro, DE, in 1938. Edith is buried here alongside her first husband, Dr. Dodds. Edith's adopted daughter married several times, raised one son in OH, before moving to Florida where she died.

If you experience some little feeling or inkling that maybe something is there, indulge yourself and take a few extra minutes to look. You might be surprised by what you find!

THOSE ANNOYING BRICK WALLS!

No matter how long one's been doing genealogy, a brick wall is going to show up eventually ... maybe more than one. .

On one visit to the Delaware Archives in Dover, I had been searching Sussex County wills for several hours; with little success. I was searching the microfilmed wills of Broadkill Hundred residents, looking specifically for any reference in them to my Stephen Carey. After all, his marriage bond had indicated that he was from Broadkill Hundred at the time he married Sophia.

Early in the search I passed up a large document (three hundred pages plus) about a James Carey. I recall thinking at the time that whoever that man was, he certainly must have had a lot of assets to divvy up if it took that many pages of a will to disperse it! Since I'd never found any information about the brother James that my William Carey said he had, I decided to check the age of this James Carey to see if he was a possible candidate.

The document turned out not to be a will at all, but a transcript of testimonies by people who knew the deceased, James Joshua Carey (or Joshua James Carey), who had been killed in 1925. Mr. Carey owned several properties in Maryland and Delaware. He spent his days walking among his many farms to make sure they were being properly cared for by the tenants who lived on each.

When elderly James Carey was found dead along a railroad track, word of his death spread quickly! One of his farm tenants rushed into Georgetown, the county seat, and immediately filed as James Joshua Carey's next-of-kin! When Mr. Carey's only "real" daughter, Mamie/Monie Baker, found out, she filed a countersuit to get this imposter removed by the courts.

This long document was the transcript of all the testimonies given by more than 100 residents of the area, some speaking on behalf of the real daughter and others supporting the farm tenant's claim. It must have been quite a circus atmosphere while all this was going on.

It took me only a few pages of reading to discover that this James Joshua Carey was 10 or more years too young to be my missing ancestor. But I always love a good mystery and this one had already piqued my interest - how was James killed? Was it an accident? Or was it murder?

The year was 1925. Poor old Joshua James Carey was the unfortunate victim who was killed. And it was murder! Like many people in that era, Joshua James Carey did not trust banks so he carried his money with him in a leather pouch. A young man in his 20's by the name of James Baker came by, saw the sleeping victim by a stack of railroad ties and knew the pouch held the old man's money! He quickly took advantage of this golden opportunity and bludgeoned Carey to death! He took the cash, threw away the pouch and raced away from the crime scene! Easy money!

As I read, I took brief notes. Witness after witness took the stand and told, under oath, told who they were, how they knew the victim or the plaintiffs in the case. On and on the stories went. Soon I felt like I knew most of the residents of southern Sussex County. The fish monger testified; so did the Watkins man. Seems that everyone knew Mr. Carey and his habits.

Testimonies droned on; but my attention span wasn't waning. Soon I'm reading the testimony of a man named Eby Carey, age 56, a nephew of the victim, and he lived near Whaleyville, MD. Eby stated he was the bastard son of James Carey's sister (unnamed, but Mary was the correct age, and his death certificate named Mary Carey as his mother). He said his biological father's last name was Murray (Ebe Murray b. 1836/wife Nancy), but he always went by the name Carey since Grandma (Elizabeth Evans) Carey raised him.

Unfortunately, by closing time, I had not read all the pages of testimony! What a disappointment! I thought the end of the story may have to wait until my next visit. After I returned home to Indiana, I contacted Helen Carey and told her about this intriguing case and asked if she could obtain any newspaper articles or other information about the crime and the surrounding events. She quickly responded with file data and copies of newspaper articles about the death of James Carey, and also a copy of Eby's death certificate. It wasn't long after that when we realized that the information gleaned from Eby's sworn testimony in 1925, when compared to the existing census and other records, helped us find the needed clue to Eby's parentage, break down that brick wall, and now allowed us to trace Horace Carey's ancestry back three more generations into the mid-1700s! What a great feeling! Who would have expected to knock down a brick wall and solve the mystery about Eby's father more than 10 years later by using testimony relating to a 1925 crime?

Although her husband has passed on, Dorothy still regularly visits the graves of Eby and his family at Crocksey Hill Cemetery near Whaleyville, MD.

FIELD TRIPS!

My research pal and cousin, Jan Pullins, accompanied me on most of my research trips to Delaware. While it's instantly gratifying to get on the internet at home and go to ancestry or some of the many other genealogy websites to search for family history, there's a lot to be said for actually visiting the sites where your relatives lived. Along the way you meet a lot of people who are willing to help you and make suggestions about local sources of data. Field trips can be very interesting, educational, and sometimes humorous!

Each year we visited with the man who currently lives at the location where the 1868 map shows our William Carey lived before leaving Delaware to come to Indiana. On our first visit to Gumboro, with clipboards in hand, we knocked on his door. He took one look and said, "Well, it's The Jehovah Witness Ladies!" And the name stuck! Every fall when we visited the area he would spot us "ladies" and just veer off the road, cross the ditch, and drive his pickup truck out to wherever we were just to say Hello! He was always interested in hearing about our discoveries!

On our last visit I'd asked if he knew of any other nearby cemeteries that we might have missed. "Yes!" He told us to go north on Pear Tree Road about 2 miles or so, look to the left and about 20-30 feet from the road we'd see a copse of trees in the cornfield. There were some graves in among those trees, he said! I asked how he learned about them, and he chuckled a bit. Said he wanted to get an early morning start the first day of deer season one year so he got up at 3 a.m., dressed warmly, took his thermos of coffee to keep himself awake. He hunkered down in among those trees and waited. When he finally got chilly enough he needed some hot coffee he turned on his light to see, yelled "Yikes," grabbed his stuff and high-tailed it out of there! The nice little snug hole he was squatting in turned out to be an open grave! He said he'd never realized and miraculously the stone had sunk almost straight down without falling either forward or backward. We were able to read and photograph it and found it was the burial site for Joshua Jarman and Esther Timmons Jarman that died around the mid-1800s. Also buried with them was one of their sons who had died rather young.

On another Fall trip, one of our earlier ones, perhaps 2005 or 2006, we noticed all these mounds of rich, black dirt in so many of the fields, waiting to be plowed under. There was one adjacent to the family cemetery we were looking for. We hiked from the road toward the cemetery. Suddenly the wind changed directions and ... SO DID WE! The rich, black dirt that we had admired? Not so -- they'd just cleaned out the chicken coops! We couldn't run away from there fast enough!

Another trip led us to the Carey Cemetery near Carey Methodist Church. We'd driven in from Fenwick Island and got there much too early for Sunday services. So we toured the cemetery and photographed Carey gravestones of interest. Then we noticed our pant legs - they were absolutely covered with tiny cockleburs! By the time we got them all picked off, we were almost late for church!

On another of our trips I returned to a cemetery that we had previously visited but now I knew a specific grave there that I wanted to photograph. Jan and I were both country and farm girls growing up so this tramping was our thing. But Jan had a quirk or two that I never failed to take advantage of. I covered the left side of the cemetery and noticed something by one of the stones. When I caught up with Jan I sent her to that specific stone because there was something really, really interesting about it. She took off while I watched and waited. I couldn't help but laugh as she came running towards the car yelling a few not-so-nice words at me! I neglected to tell her a couple things - like the dry snake skin that had been shed by the snake wrapping him-- or herself around the stone until its skin finally came off, and the minor fact that the dried skin was a good 10-12 feet long! Jan had a good memory, however. She never ever got out of the car at that cemetery again!

Field trips can be a lot of fun. But they're also helpful in establishing family groups that are buried in plots. Often you can learn other collateral family names faster and easier this way than searching by computer. And with today's do-every-thing phones, taking a picture is a snap- literally.

And if you are fortunate enough to discover a wonderful group of people researching your particular surname(s), go meet them! It is wonderful to share your data, photos, family history and ideas, as you listen and learn from the others! Thank you so very much, Niel and Helen Carey, for creating The Carey/Cary Family Reunion!

Now, get out of your computer chair and go find your ancestors. Happy hunting!

- Diane Hanson

Retired engineer and quality project manager; Perdue University graduate; Draftswoman, technical publications editor, magazine associate editor, quality engineer; Note: Genealogy and history is a lot more fun than working for a living!

William H. Carey
1840-1916

CHAPTER 6

MY CAREY/CARY FAMILY FROM THE EASTERN SHORE OF MARYLAND TO ERATH COUNTY, TX
- REX AND JANICE CAREY -

Hearing the slide action of a pump shotgun focuses your attention very quickly, particularly when you hear it on the other side of a door you have just knocked on... In Sept 1963 my wife, Janice Elaine Koonsman Carey, our three month old daughter, Kristy LuAnn Carey, and I were on our way from Stephenville, TX, to McGuire AFB, New Jersey, to catch a plane to Frankfurt, Germany on an Air Force assignment when we stopped at a relative's house a few miles East of Nashville, AR, in Hempstead County. Kristy LuAnn was later joined by her sister, Jill Suzanne Carey, and brother, Joel Lynn Carey. The relative was my Grandpa Carey's (John Henry Carey) oldest sister's daughter and her husband. They did not know we were coming. It was at night with darkness compounded by the pine trees around 8 o'clock when I knocked on the door. After a few seconds I heard footsteps, then the sound of a slide action on the shotgun, with which I was very familiar.

Fortunately I thought to let them know very quickly that my Dad was Fred Carey, who was a cousin of the lady of the house and someone they knew. Those were the magic words since the porch light came on, and we were invited in for a great overnight visit. They put us up for the night, gave us a tour of the family-related places in the area and provided a breakfast with some of the best biscuits and gravy available anywhere. We found out that the man of the house, who was a carpenter/builder in addition to being a farmer, had just been paid and was concerned about their safety.

My Mother, Vonzeal Suitt Carey, wrote our hosts a month or two later and obtained a good start on a family tree for the Carey family, as they were aware of at the time. Earlier, as a youngster, I had asked my Dad and Grandpa about the family history. Grandpa Carey provided the name of his father, Jasper Carey, 1848–1882, and his grandfather, Daniel Carey, 1808–abt 1882.

Grandpa Carey and his wife, Nancy Elizabeth Hipp Carey, went to Erath County, Texas, to the Oakdale Community north of Stephenville, TX, in 1902 with their two oldest children, Ada and Emma. Later, Effie, Emmitt, my Dad Fred Carey, and Verna were born. They moved there from Hempstead County, AR, a few miles East of Nashville, AR, where we first visited 61 years later. Nashville is in Howard County which was carved out of Hempstead County in 1873. Grandpa Carey and family moved from the Oakdale Community to the Selden Community, about ten miles south of Stephenville, TX, in 1917.

Selden is the community where my parents, Fred Naylor Carey and Vonzeal Suitt Carey lived with my brother Kenneth Vaughan Carey and myself. Our parents did general farming raising cotton, corn, oats, feed grains, along with turkeys, chickens and milk cows. In 1951 the farming operation converted to primarily a Grade A dairy operation as was the case with a number of our neighbors. The community had a school for grades 1 throught 8. After the 8th grade students were bussed into Stephenville, about ten miles away. There were

Baptist and Methodist churches along with a general store and a cotton gin, the last operating cotton gin in the Erath County.

Jasper Carey and wife, Nancy Elizabeth Stone Carey Lewis, between 1870 and 1882, had Mary Elizabeth Carey, Willie Ann Carey, George Washington Carey, John Henry Carey, Jocie Carey, Robert G. Carey, Sarah Emma Carey and Samuel Newton Carey. Jasper Newton Carey died on 20 Sept 1882 from yellow fever.

After returning to Texas from our assignment in West Germany in Sept 1966 to another in Austin, TX, i. e., to school and then work with the U. S. Office of Economic Opportunity in Austin, TX, we moved to Duncanville, TX, near Dallas in 1971. I started working more on the family history. The Dallas Public Library in downtown Dallas had, and continues to have, an outstanding genealogical library. Lloyd Bockstruck was the director for a number of years and also conducted genealogical workshops which I had the good fortune to attend. The Dallas Library microfiche files with census information, together with federal land sale information, helped me connect the family from Hempstead County, AR, to Henderson County, TN, where they were living when Daniel Carey moved the family to Hempstead County, AR, about 1851.

Daniel Carey and Sarah Howard Cannon Carey had eight children between 1835 and 1854 with James Carey, Eliza Jane Carey, William Henry Carey, George Carey, Rufus Carey, Jasper Newton Carey, Albert A. Carey born in TN and John W. Carey born in Arkansas. Census and land records also helped identify Daniel as being born in Orange County, NC, followed by a move to Henderson County, TN, about 1821 with his father Michael Carey and wife Leah Ennis. Census information indicated that Michael Carey was born in Maryland on the

Eastern Shore.

Due to work trips to the Washington DC area we were able to visit family history- related locations en route on occasion in Alabama, Arkansas, Tennessee, North Carolina and Maryland. On our first trip to the Eastern Shore we stopped at a library, I think, was in Salisbury, MD, asking for who might be working on the Carey Family and was directed to Mary Frances Carey, in New Church, VA, who had done a good deal of work on the family of her husband, William C. Carey. Mary Frances' research indicated that Michael Carey left the Eastern Shore in 1795. The research that I had done in Orange County, NC, showed Michael buying land there in 1795.

Mary Frances' research further indicated that Michael Carey's parents were Thomas Carey, (b. around 1733) and Margaret Raglin. However, some researchers concluded that Michael's father was William based on the suffix, Jr., on a sibling's name. However, it should be noted that the Jr. suffix can signify a younger relative with the same name, not necessarily a son—perhaps a nephew. Due to this, along with the naming patterns in the family of Michael, Mary Frances concluded that Thomas was the father of Michael.

Her research further showed that Thomas Carey's father was Levin Carey, b. circa 1708 and d. in Worcester County, MD, in 1783. Levin Carey's father was William Carey, Sr., b. on 10 May 1668 in Somerset Co., MD, d. 1734, with wife Elizabeth. William Carey, Sr's father was Thomas Cary of Monye Creek, Somterset Co., MD, b. 1610 – 1620. His name first appeared in MD records in 1666.

Mary Frances' research indicates that Thomas Cary and his wife Jane appear in Somerset County, MD, soon after it was established on 22 Aug 1666. He had surveyed three hundred acres of land on the north side of Great Monye Creek in Somerset on 20 Nov 1666 (Som. Co. Rent Rolls of 1723). This tract of land was called Cary's Adventure, and in the entry for his right to it, on 10 Jan 1671, Thomas named himself; his wife, Jane; Edward, Thomas and John, his children; and Alexander Ferrill, his servant (MD Land Patents 316, p. 537). These six people entitled him to the three hundred acres for their transport into Maryland from Virginia. The patent was issued on 20 February 1673.

On 11 November 1674, Thomas Cary bought one hundred fifty additional acres called Washford from Henry Hayman and his wife, Eleanor (Som. Co. Deeds#4, p. 132). This tract was adjacent to Cary's Adventure and just east of it. (Reference: *Thomas Cary of Monye Creek and Worcester County Maryland, and Descendants*, Mary Frances Carey, 1983.)

Mary Frances concluded that most likely Thomas Cary had emigrated from Virginia to the Eastern Shore and was the one given a headright by Col. Richard Lee, after which he patented three hundred acres in Lancaster County, VA on 14 Nov 1653. She states that this Thomas Cary would have had time to work out an indenture, marry, and father children by the time he appeared in Somerset County, Maryland.

My wife and I have benefitted from membership in the Erath County Genealogical Society, for which I wrote an article on the Selden Community in the April 2014 edition of their Journal, pp. 38 – 52. We are also members of the Ellis County Genealogical Society which meets in Waxahachie, TX, in our home county, monthly during the winter. This provides an opportunity to help keep up to date on resources and techniques involved in genealogy.

We have done DNA testing with Family Tree DNA, both

Y and mtdna, and are members of the Carey/Cary Family Organization. We have also done DNA testing with Ancestry. com.

My wife, Janice, and I did a cleanup and fencing in 2005 - 2006 of the Bateman Cemetery near Nashville, AR, where Jasper Carey, his wife, Nancy Elizabeth Stone Carey Lewis, several members in their family and a large number of relatives are buried. We continue to work with the land owners to ensure the cemetery is maintained. Following is a link to the Bateman Cemetery website. https://arkansasgravestones.org/cemetery.php?cemID=8458

Additionally, I have served on the Ellis County Historical Commisssion for several years. We did an update on the cemetery listings for the county with GPS locations for those that were missing for the Texas Dept. of Transportation in their I-35 Project. This project was conducted in 2009 – 2010.

My mother, Vonzeal Suitt Carey, was born in Selden in 1913. Her father, Lieneous Tyre Suitt, born in Praire County, AR, in 1879, moved with his family from AR to a farm near Selden in 1892 shortly after his father, William Alexander Suitt, b. 1831, had passed away due to pneumonia contracted while hiding out in the woods from the KKK. He and other farmers were holding their hogs off the market in protest against some of the harsh lending practices of the town merchants who paid a visit in retaliation.

William Alexander Suitt was one of the organizers of the Agricultural Wheel, a farmer's advocacy group, which later merged with the Farmer's Alliance. He was born in Lauderdale Co., AL, moved to Tennessee and on to Prairie Co., Arkansas, around 1856. His wife, Eliza Elizabeth Faitha Fields was born near Lydia, SC, before moving to AR around 1870. My mother's mother was Eula Belle Stone, b. in 1891, whose father, Hiram Avery Stone and mother Dovie Ellen Long moved from AL to the Salem Community near Selden in abt 1874.

My wife's father was William Henry (W. H.) Koonsman, b. 1917, son of Charlie James Koonsman and Edna Ardena Wolfe d. 1918, and whose great grandfather, Jacob Koonsman, and wife, Sophia Hite Koonsman, had moved to a farm in the Salem Community south of Selden about 1874 from West VA. They moved to West VA from PA where they had previously arrived from Germany. Charlie James Koonsman, son of William Edward Koonsman and Elizabeth Evelyn Hawkins, later married Emmett Ward.

My wife's mother, Rossie Pauline Koonsman, b. 1917, was daughter of Lonnie Judson Frost, farmer and minister, and Mattie Rossie Shackleford, who lived in the community of Lake Creek in Haskell County, TX, before moving to Erath County south of the Selden Community in the early 1940s.

- Rex and Janice Carey

Janice Elaine Koonsman Carey – born in 1943 in Erath County, TX. Selden Elementary School, Stephenville High School, Tarleton State College, Mt. View College, University of Texas at Arlington, BS and MS in Social Work. Real Estate Sales and Dir. of REACH, substance abuse program.

Rex Lynn Carey – born in 1939 in Erath County, TX. Selden Elementary School, Stephenville High Schoool, Tarleton State College, Baylor University, University of Texas at Austin, BA in history and MA in government. US Air Force; US Office of Economic Opportunity; Dept. of Navy; Dept. of Agriculture, Food and Nutrition Service.

CHAPTER 7

CAREYS IN PENNSYLVANIA
FROM PLYMOUTH PILGRIM TO CALIFORNIA
- CECILY MARBLE HINTZEN -

Introduction

John Miner Carey Marble (JMCM) is my second great-grandfather. This photograph was one of a collection of family photographs in our upstairs hallway which, through the years, inspired a natural interest in my roots. The photograph depicts JMCM, with his son, Guilford Lionel Marble and Guilford's wife, Cora May Depuy, with their sons, John McKinley Marble and my grandfather, William Baird Marble.

My mother, Margaret Duque Marble, did extensive genealogical research on her family and my father's family. After her death, my brother, Baird, and I have continued her exploration. With the advent of the internet, our research has yielded a trove of information my mother did not have the skills to access, still she gleaned much from her research travels. JMCM himself was dedicated to researching his family and we have published evidence of his endeavors.

ORIGINS

John Miner Carey Marble (1833-1912) was the only surviving son of Hannah Carey (1808-1888) and Ebenezer Marble. He was born in Luzerne County, Pennsylvania, the seat of this branch of the Carey family since 1769 when Eleazer Carey (1718-1779) came to the Wyoming Valley, on the Susquehanna River, as one of the first forty settlers. There he established a township known as Careytown in the lower part of what is now Wilkes-Barre. Eleazer was the son of Samuel Cary (1677-1759), who had moved his family from Bridgewater, Massachusetts, to Duchess County, New York, where Eleazer was born. Samuel was the eldest son of Francis Cary (1647-1718), the son of John Cary (1610-1681) and Elizabeth Godfrey (1620-1680), the subject of Seth Cary's work John Cary, the Plymouth Pilgrim.

I have been able to confirm this lineage with DNA through to John Carey (1756-1844), the son of Eleazer Carey. I have learned that the more distant cousins one can find, the further back you can confirm your DNA connection to your ancestors. So, it is worthwhile to reach out to your fifth through eighth cousins.

Proceeding from the assumption that John Cary and Elizabeth Godfrey are the true progenitors of my family line, I am highly confident that the Marble-Carey branch descends from John's son, Francis Cary in America. I am further convinced that the Delaware-Maryland-Virginia line probably originated with a brother or cousin of John Cary, the "pilgrim," but I have not done enough research to support this hypothesis.

John Cary[1] (pilgrim) arrived in 1634 and settled in Bridgewater, Plymouth Colony. His son, Francis, was so named to honor his grandfather, Francis Godfrey. Most of the records indicate that Francis married a Hannah Brett and a controversy has arisen over whether his wife was Hannah or her sister, Lydia. An article in the American Genealogist (v.61, no.3, p129-132) disputes the accuracy of all the secondary source records including Brett Genealogy. (Part 1:38, 52-53), Torrey's New England Marriages Prior to 1700 [Baltimore 19851 (p.134), Mitchell's Bridgewater (p. 132), and Seth Cary's John Cary the Plymouth Pilgrim (Boston 1911) (p. 64) and presents evidence that Francis married Lydia Brett. I don't believe that the distinction affects who his children were.

Francis[2] had five children. His eldest, Samuel[3] (1677-1759), was named to honor Samuel Tompkins who bequeathed his estate in East Bridgewater to Francis. Samuel married Mary Poole in 1704 who gave birth to nine children. Samuel relocated his family to Dover, Duchess County, New York, where he died at the age of 82.

Eleazer Cary[4] (1718-1779) was the eldest son of Samuel, born in Bridgewater, and moved with the family to Dover, New York. There he married Charity Sturdevant, although I can find no record that supports this. JMCM wrote extensively about Samuel Carey and he had six children. Eleazer's second son, John Carey[5] (1756-1844) is my ancestor confirmed by DNA. In 1759 Eleazer joined the Connecticut 3rd Regiment, 1st Company under the command of Colonel and Captain Eleazer Fitch to fight in the French-Indian war. It must have been at this time he became involved with Susquehanna Company of Connecticut and became one of the first forty pioneers to settle the Wyoming Valley in Pennsylvania. Records show that his son John, then fifteen years old, accompanied him. His family soon followed and there they put down roots in Careytown, named for him, in the lower part of what is now Wilkes-Barre. It wasn't until after his death that his claim to the township was made official. He was buried in the Cary burying ground, where the St. Clement's Church now stands on Hanover Street.

JMCM tells the harrowing story of Eleazer's third son, Samuel, who at the age of nineteen, joined the company of a Captain Bidlack to defend their Wyoming Valley settlement against the invasion by native Indians hired by the English and Tories in what came to be known as the Massacre of Wyoming. Samuel was captured by the Indians and was subsequently adopted to replace the son lost in one of the battles. He was aided in his attempt to escape by his adoptive mother, but he was recaptured and ultimately sold to the British. After peace was negotiated, he was traded for a British prisoner and returned home June 29, 1784, after an absence of six years.

> It is said the men were nearly a mile away from the house, working in the field. A messenger hastened, not by telegraph or telephone or steam or electricity, but as fast as his limbs would carry him, and on receipt of the news the men dropped their tools and hastened to meet and greet him who had long been counted as dead, but behold,

was present and still alive. The sudden outburst of joy that filled and thrilled the hearts of his family, we think, was greater than that showed by Jacob and sons when they met in Egypt, or that of the father on the return of his prodigal son. (Marble, Samuel Carey p.10)

But, I digress, as Samuel is not my direct ancestor, his older brother John is. John Carey[5] was born in Bond's Bridge, New York, before moving to the Wyoming Valley. He served in the Continental Army during the Revolutionary War, attaining the rank of Corporal in Captain Thomas Craig's Company of the second Battalion commanded by Colonel Wood. Family lore says that he was known as the Samson of the company and that he was with Washington at Valley Forge, but I have not yet found evidence of this. John married the widow Susanna Green, the mother of all his children. When he died, he was buried in Wilkes-Barre with military honors.

John's eldest son, John Carey[6] (1783-1808) married Katharine "Kitty" Vandermark, pictured below, when he was eighteen years old. He had five children, only three surviving to adulthood. His youngest was Hannah Carey[7] (1808-1888), whose marriage to Ebenezer Marble marks the beginning of the Marble-Carey line. According to Seth Carey in *John Cary: The Plymouth Pilgrim*, "The Marbles and Carys were of good New England stock, were moral and religious, most of them being Methodists." (p. 118)

Ebenezer and Hannah had two children, Theodore, who died at the age of two, and John Miner Carey Marble[8] (1833-1912), my second great-grandfather. JMCM was named after his grandfather, John, and one of his sons, Miner Carey, who died at the age of three. John's father died soon after his

Katherine Vandermark Carey   Hannah Carey Marble

birth, most likely fighting the Indians. As of this writing, there is no record of the circumstances that led to his death, but it is believed he died in Rhode Island. Hannah retreated to the home of her grandfather, John Carey[5], her own father having died in 1808, the year she was born. Thus, it is no wonder that JMCM felt a strong affinity for his Carey roots, declaring that his great grandfather was virtually a father to him until he died in 1844. (Smith, *Eleazer Cary Family*, p. 9)

In November 1846, Hannah and John migrated to Ohio where her widowed mother had made a home with her second husband, Jacob Rimer. JMCM proved to be industrious and business savvy culminating in the establishment of the First National Bank of Delphos. He was heavily involved in the area's business interests, securing industries such as the Delphos Union Stave company and the Ohio Wheel company. A neighborhood in Delphos called Marbletown was named in his honor. He and his family moved to neighboring Van Wert, where his eldest son, Guilford Lionel Marble[9] (1862-1902) was born with first wife Mary Elizabeth "Lizzie" Coleman. She died in 1863.

John Miner Carey Marble

Mary Elizabeth "Lizzie" Coleman

During the War of the Rebellion (Civil War), the Ohio National Guard was called into action and JMCM served as Colonel, assigned to the Allen county regiment, later consolidated with the Hocking county regiment to form the 151st regiment and was mustered into federal service to be stationed in Washington, D.C., where his troops were instrumental in defending the national capital.

After the war, he married Elizabeth Emerson, who bore him three more children. JMCM engaged in many business enterprises with his new father-in-law including the private banking house of Emerson, Marble & Co., which later became the Van Wert National Bank in 1883. In 1888, the family moved to California, where he formed the National Bank of California, formed the California chapter of the Sons of the American Revolution, and avidly researched his family history.

Guilford Lionel Marble[9] became a prominent attorney in Van Wert. He married Lenore Kate Sherwood in 1887 and fathered one child, Katherine Sherwood Marble. The marriage ended and Lenore removed to California with her daughter.

Guilford Lionel Marble Latchford

Cora May Depuy Marble

Guilford then married Cora May Depuy in 1894 and had two children: John McKinley Marble and William Baird Marble[10] (1901-1956), my grandfather.

Like his father before him, Guilford was associated with many business concerns in Ohio, including the Jackson and Mackinaw Railroad, the Edison Mutual Telegraph Company (later absorbed by Western Union), the Electric Light Works in Van Wert and considerable oil interests. He was honored as a delegate to the 1892 Republican convention in support of William McKinley.

Guilford was afflicted with neurasthenia and alternated time between conducting business in Ohio and seeking treatment and rest in California. Letters between him and his father suggest that their relationship was strained over his condition. Guilford died at the age of 40, leaving his sons effectively fatherless until their mother married William Jolee Latchford in 1903. That is now three generations of sons whose fathers were absent in their upbringing.

We come now to the most recent generations of Carey cousins many of whom still use the Carey name. My brother

John Miner Carey Marble II is named for JMCM. My cousin Carey Lewis is named in recognition of her heritage. The surnames affiliated with the Carey continues to grow and connecting with them and their DNA may possibly bring us closer to understanding our lineage for many centuries that precede us.

CAREY OR CARY?

In his essay, *Samuel Carey: Participant in the Massacre of Wyoming, July 2, 1778, and Six Years a Prisoner with British and Indians*, JMCM explored the spelling of Carey:

> The transitions of the name [have] been many vis., : Kari, Karry, Cari, Caree, Carye, Carew, Carey and Cary, the "de" being used in several generations.
>
> The most common form in this day is Carey and Cary though there has been no uniformity even in some of the closely related families in the spelling.
>
> The family that the writer is closely related to, uniformly, so far as he has discovered, before and during the Revolutionary wars, used the long form Carey, but many of the same families have later dropped the "e". In what follows, the write adopts the mode used by his mother. (p.4)
>
> That part of the family, that were among the first settlers of Wyoming Valley and that permanently remained there, to whom the writer was related, in spelling the name used the long form C-a-r-e-y, and therefore in this paper that form is generally conformed to. (p.5).

Thus, the spelling preferred by the Pennsylvania branch, is CAREY and the practice has among the Carey cousins of California, of which I am a member.

- Cecily Marble Hintzen

BA, History, University of California, Santa Barbara; MS, Counseling & Guidance, California Lutheran University

I am the eldest surviving child of seven children born to William Baird Marble Jr., the son of the infant pictured on the first page and my mother, Margaret Duque Marble. I have three brothers: William Baird Marble III, Thomas Fleming Marble, and John Miner Carey Marble II; and I have 2 sisters Amanda Louise Marble and Margaret Mary Marble. We all live in California, except for Amanda who lives near Portland, Oregon. My daughter, Hillary Hintzen Greenwald and her husband David also live in Portland, Oregon with their two children, Joni Margot and Samuel Parker. My husband John and I will have been married 40 years in May 2020.

My father had two sisters: Cynthia Marble Howes and Sarah Marble Lewis. Cynthia (Mimi) also had seven children, six of whom survived to adulthood: Cynthia Howes Kepner, Dana Howes Anderson, Benjamin Durward Howes IV, Mary Devin Starratt, Brett Howes Hunter, and Briant Davidson Howes. Sarah (Sally) had four children: Carey Lewis Mott, Thomas Joseph Lewis, Julia Lewis Bullock, and Mary Rebecca Lewis.

BIBLIOGRAPHY

A portrait and biographical record of Allen and Van Wert Counties, Ohio: Containing biographical sketches of many prominent and representative citizens, together with biographies and portraits of all the presidents of the United States, and biographies of the governors of Ohio. (1896). Chicago, IL: A.W. Bowen.

Bradsby, H. C. (Ed.). (1893). *History of Luzerne County, Pennsylvania: With biographical selections.* Chicago, IL: S. B. Nelson.

Cary, Henry Grosvenor (1907). The Cary Family in America. Boston, MA: Press of Murray & Emery Company.

Cary, S. C. (1911). John Cary the Plymouth Pilgrim. Boston, MA: Seth C. Cary.

Clegg, M. L. (n.d.). Francis Cary's, b. 1647, wife? Retrieved July 31, 2019, from http://www.advsolutions.com/carey/controversy.htm

Finter, R. (January/April 1986). John Turner and Francis Cary of Bridgewater, Mass., and their wives Hannah and Lydia Brett. *The American Genealogist*, 61(3), 243rd ser., 129-132. Retrieved July 31, 2019.

Harvey, O. J. (1974). *A history of Wilkes-Barre, Luzerne County, Pennsylvania: From its first beginnings to the present time, including chapters of newly discovered early Wyoming Valley history, together with many biographical sketches and much genealogical material.* Tucson, AZ: W.C. Cox.

Marble, John Miner Carey. *Samuel Carey: Participant in the Massacre of Wyoming, July 3, 1778 and Six Years a Prisoner with the British and Indians.* New England Historical Genealogy Society.

Mitchell, N. (1897). *Mitchells History of Bridgewater, Massachusetts.* Bridgewater, MA: E. Alden.

Smith, A. C. (1744-1820). *Eleazer Cary Family with Affiliated Lines also Items of Interest to other lines* [PDF]. www.internetarchive.org. Published by Mrs. A.C. Smith, historian of the Eleazer Cary Family and past president of Cary Family Association of Wyoming and Lackawanna Counties, for the purpose of corrections and further information; then to be published in a larger edition

CHAPTER 8

THE CAREYS OF MILLSBORO
- ED CAREY -

It is not always that we aspire to do a great thing. Moreover, it is simply in striving to do that which is placed before us that greatness is revealed.

My grandfather, Elijah E. Carey, was the only child of Elijah W. and his second wife Lavinia E. Mears. Born February 24, 1876, he would grow up working on his father's farm. The Carey family farm was comprised of several tracts of land totaling approximately 300 acres, extending out from the present day location of Carey's Camp, in what would be the farm's southeast corner. Conway Road which today intersects Careys Camp Road did not exist. There was no road through the farm north to Phillips Hill Road or south to Mission.

With the passing of his father, in 1887, when he was just eleven, young Elijah Edward would learn all too quickly some of life's tough lessons. His mother certainly understood the burdens that would come with trying to manage a large farming operation of the day, and within a year of the passing of Elijah W., the bulk of the farmland was being sold.

Not much is recorded as to Elijah Edward's activities from that time until 1897, when in October of that year, at the age of twenty-one, he established a mercantile business in Shortly, about four miles north of the farm. In that same year he married Mary L. Wharton, also of Shortly, and in 1898, a son, Leroy (Lee), was born to the couple. A second child was born in November of 1900 who survived for just one hour. Sadly, this would mark the beginning of a pattern that was to plague the Careys.

By 1901, grandfather had relocated to Millsboro, forming a partnership with his father-in-law, operating under the name of Carey & Wharton, and during which time a third child, Mary E., had come along. In 1902, the couple was blessed with a second daughter, Edna M., only to suffer the loss of Mary in 1904 to measles. Edna would pass away from causes unknown in 1905.

Grandfather Carey continued with the Carey & Wharton business until sometime in 1905 when Mr. Wharton sold his interest to Walter P. Monroe who would later operate a clothing store, in a partnership with his brother, in downtown Millsboro.

By 1906 another daughter, Mildred, was born to Ed (as he now referred to himself) and Mary. However, the child was not to see her first year and passed away later in 1906.

On October 6, 1907, another daughter, Bertha Eleanor, was

born, and although her prospects for survival held promise, her formative years would not be without anxiety and suffering from the effects of tuberculosis, known as "consumption" in those days. By the beginning of the 19th century, tuberculosis killed one in seven of all those who had ever lived.

Ed and Mary began married life living in Shortly and at some point built a house on the corner of today's Morris and Church Streets. Grandfather continued in the business partnership of general merchandise with Walter Monroe as Carey & Monroe until about 1911, at which time he began conducting business solely in his own name, continuing for two more years.

In 1913, he was appointed postmaster by President Woodrow Wilson, continuing in that position until 1922, all the while operating his mercantile business and even forming a new partnership, Carey & Truitt. This operation continued until sometime in 1925. Following the business partnership of Carey & Truitt, in 1925, grandfather began a farming, trucking, and retail coal business under the name of Carey & McGee.

On January 4, 1914, another child was born to Ed and Mary, only to survive until May of that same year, and as if all the losses grandfather had experienced at this point could not possibly be enough, his beloved wife Mary would pass away on January 9, 1915.

World War I had begun in 1914, but America did not enter until April 2, 1917. We know that grandfather's first son, Lee, served in the army during that period but have no knowledge as to where his service may have taken him or what his experiences may have been. I have his helmet somewhere in my collection.

On December 26, 1917, grandfather married Bessie B.

Johnson of Millsboro. Bessie had grown up in the family home built by her father, William Johnson, a blacksmith, in 1884, on what was then Morris Avenue, just across the street from the Carey home. Great-grandfather Johnson's blacksmith shop was in the building behind the house, and opened onto Central Alley behind. I vividly remember visiting the remains of the old forge many times when I was growing up, while spending countless hours with my then widowed grandmother and my Aunt Ann.

On Saturday, the 26th of July, 1919, Grandfather Carey's only surviving daughter, Bertha, passed away at Hope Farm, later known as Emily Bissell, located in New Castle County, a facility constructed for the sole purpose of treating tuberculosis.

Death certificates were not always issued in those bygone days, and the causes of death of the other children of Ed and Mary are not all known. We can only speculate as to the effects of this dreaded disease and how it may have impacted the other family members.

The widespread use of formal birth certificates was not in place back then with most such recording performed carefully on a front page of ever-present and very large family bibles. In the cases of those Carey children who survived only hours or days, no names are recorded, the sex of the child is not known, and places of interment are not documented. The three young girls who were named are buried at Carey's Cemetery, in what was originally the family cemetery of Elijah W. Carey. Bertha is buried in Millsboro Cemetery, then known as Brotherhood, as is her mother, Mary.

On April 23, 1921, a son, Elijah E. Carey, Jr. (E. Edward, Ned) was born in the family home on the corner of Church and Morris Streets, and on June 22nd the following year, a daughter, Ann Elizabeth, was also born at home. Recorded in the cement sidewalk approaching the side porch of the house were Dad's and Aunt Ann's initials and their dates of birth. I have always regretted not having mentioned something to the new owners when I had the opportunity. The porch disappeared in a renovation as did that small section of sidewalk.

Lee was married to Evaleah Lance Green on June 2, 1923, and they are remembered to have made their home in the Georgetown area. Just five years later, on October 27th, 1928, grandfather's only surviving child from his first family, Lee, passed away at the Georgetown home of his in-laws. Grandfather was reported to have collapsed at Lee's funeral.

Just how long grandfather continued in the partnership with Mr. McGee is unclear, but by 1928 he had become an insurance agent for the United States Fidelity and Guaranty Company. In that year he was also elected Mayor of Millsboro, a position he held for several years. Although perhaps unsolicited, his presence in the town's mayoral office provided ready accessibility for his insurance clients. This worked to his disadvantage politically, however, as some evidently took exception to the practice and it eventually cost him an election.

Grandfather was also involved in a business venture with two other men that made him part owner of a tomato cannery on Old Landing Road. It would later become the Millsboro Poultry plant, just across the street from present-day Merck Company. Dad worked in the cannery as a young boy, making 10-cents an hour; great money at the time.

In 1937, grandfather was appointed Deputy State Treasurer by Dr. Blackstone, who had just been elected to the Office of Treasurer. Dr. Blackstone was a local pharmacist, operating his business in the building in which Carey's Frame Shop is now located, and in that earlier time a popular political gathering place.

In the early 40s, a property that contained a house and a general store became available on Laurel Road, two miles west of Millsboro. Grandfather and Grandmother purchased the property, a move that allowed him to resume his business pursuits. It also allowed him to have his insurance agency in his own space, located in a separate room of the residence.

They are believed to have sold the Morris Street house at this time to a lady always known to all of us as Aunt Elsie Wharton. She is thought to have been related somehow to Grandfather's first wife, and was living there as far back as I can remember.

Grandmother had inherited the Johnson Property and she rented it to a young undertaker, Ronald James, who was then in the formative days of his funeral business. Viewings were actually held at the house with coffins passed through the front porch window of what was then the parlor.

By 1939 the world was at war, and with the Japanese attack on Pearl Harbor in 1941, young Ned Carey, my father, just twenty years old, began making his plans for military service, but not before marrying Beatrice Mae Wells of Milton on August 1, 1942. Dad's service in the Army Air Corps kept him stateside in training squadrons, serving at Shaw Field in Sumter, South Carolina, and in Lincoln, Nebraska.

In 1944, Grandfather Carey suffered a heart attack, whereupon Dad was summoned home and was subsequently granted an early discharge in order to help his mother with the family business. Dad and Mother rented the Johnson property from Grandmother Carey and set about preparing their new home for an addition. On the morning of October 30, 1944, a son was born to the couple, Elijah Edward Carey, III, yours truly.

Sadly, that evening, Grandfather Carey passed away. His life was filled with many challenges and much grief. Whether his entrepreneurial spirit was driven from desire or necessity, no one knows. We do know that he must have sustained serious financial burdens arising from the medical and funeral costs of the day. My mother has told me often that she never heard a single complaint from him, and how impressed she was of his calm resilient demeanor. He was just 68.

Grandmother Carey exchanged residences with Mom and Dad as they assumed full responsibility of the general store business, sometime in 1945. From my time growing up there, I clearly remember the shelves lined with canned goods, the glass front meat case, the butcher block, the cold storage room, the gas pumps, the pickle barrel, and farm machinery. I also recall clandestine trips to the ice cream and cold soda cases, more than one of which ended in temporary banishment.

Having relocated back to town, to the Johnson property, Grandmother continued with the insurance agency which grandfather had established. I spent a lot of hours with grandmother and my Aunt Ann who had continued to live at home with her mother. Aunt Ann had had serious plans for Flight Officer Morton Donaway when he went away into the service, but he was killed during a bombing raid over Italy on April 10, 1945. Consequently, Aunt Ann remained single for quite a few more years after that loss. All of this was to my advantage, however, as I never lacked for great experiences.

In 1948, my brother, William Frederick (Fred) came along, and we shared many happy childhood days together growing up and running practically free-range in the country, and later, in much the same fashion, in small town Millsboro.

A country general store may conjure up nostalgic thoughts and visions - it does with me - I lived it, but for a husband and wife team who are married to it as well as to each other, the long hours are a grind, and by 1950, Mom and Dad were making plans for something else.

As 1953 dawned, Carey's Paint & Hardware was making a colorful addition to downtown Millsboro. The building was sporting the bright orange and white colors of the Athey Paint Company of Baltimore, and Mom and Dad were open for business. The Laurel Road store was sold to the Mumfords who operated a business there until the 1970s.

On October 19, 1951, Ann married Clayton McCabe Dukes of Selbyville. They would start married life in Millsboro and eventually move to New Castle, to be nearer to his work. Aunt Anne and Uncle Clayton would raise two sons, Clayton, Jr., and Bill.

In 1961, Grandmother Carey passed away at the home of Ann and Clayton. Dad and Mom bought the Johnson property and set to making renovations to what would become our new home by late 1962.

Over the years, Dad served the community of Millsboro in many ways. He is remembered by many for his devotion to the fire service and by still others for the life-saving dashes he made as a volunteer driver in the local ambulance squad. Mother was very supportive of his efforts and filled his vacant spot in the store whenever the alarm for help was sounded in our community.

Dad worked outside the shop in various ways, and one in particular provided many unique experiences for me. We were very good friends with a local funeral director, and the business end of that relationship enabled me to put a value on mortality at an early age. I went with Dad many times when he would be called to assist to transport someone. Dad would eventually serve as Deputy Coroner when the funeral director was elected to the post in the 60s.

For many years, Mother wrote for several local newspapers as the Millsboro social editor and provided what we always teasingly referred to as the "gossip column". Her Royal typewriter sits today as a quiet reminder of the many nights it filled the air with its clickety-clack keyboard and ding-dinging carriage return, the social media machine of a bygone day.

Never lacking for an outlet in his desire to serve, Dad would be appointed Town Alderman during the 70s. The many cases that came before him added a colorful flavor to dinner time conversations and provided an otherwise unknown insight into community happenings.

Bea and Ned Carey

Mom and Dad developed a loyal customer base with the paint and hardware business, and over time increased the diversity as they added lines arising from hobbies in which they each had developed interests. Mother had taken up painting, and soon the store was experiencing an influx of customers from the local art community. Dad acquired a horse (and later two more for Fred and me), and this interest led to the addition of saddlery.

By the mid-sixties, Mom and Dad were feeling the effects of competition from a new store in town that was part of a regional chain that sold the very same line of paint. Understanding the situation that Mom and Dad were in, but powerless to do anything directly, the paint company sales representative encouraged them to look into custom picture framing. This business line became their crowning glory and Carey's Paint and Frame Shoppe was well-known throughout the area. In the 80s, they added a limited line of paint products under the Devoe label.

Dad passed away in 2004, and Mom continued to operate the business until health deterred her in 2016. After a brief period of inactivity, I reopened the store doing business as Carey's Frame Shop in May 2017 and in 2018, added lamp repair.

After working for the L. D. Caulk Company in Milford and living there for about twenty years, I moved back to help Mother, a situation which also put me closer to my daughters' families and six wonderful grandchildren. My brother retired from the postal service several years ago and lives a few miles outside of Millsboro. Fred and his wife have a daughter and two grandchildren.

With the passage of time, the "Careys of Millsboro" will ultimately become just a memory, as any hope of carrying the name forward sadly disappeared with the untimely death of the last male in our line, my brother's son, just a few years ago. But, those offspring even without the family name, both now and in the future, nevertheless follow with Carey blood in their veins and can claim the legacy of the Carey/Cary line with justifiable pride. May they in turn give each successive generation reason to be proud of their contributions to the Carey legacy.

- Ed Carey

Ed Carey grew up in Millsboro and received his formal education in the public school system, and was among the first to complete training in electronics at a then new technical school, in Sussex County. Upon graduation he continued his training in electronics technology at Capitol Radio Engineering Institute, in Washington, DC. He subsequently entered military service in the United States Air Force, receiving specialized training in electronics technology and in guided missile systems. Ed married the former Ann Brumley of Georgetown in 1967, and continued his military service for eight years, at various locations. Upon leaving the Air Force with his growing family of two daughters, he became a licensed insurance agent and built a home in Georgetown. Ed and his wife were divorced in 1983. He served as the Director of Emergency Operations for Sussex County from 1987 to 1992. Following his time with the county, he worked for the L. D. Caulk Company of Milford, where he lived until his retirement in 2009. Ed currently resides in Millsboro. He is a member of the Carey/Cary Family organization and made a presentation at one of our reunions entitled "The Careys of Sussex or what I learned about my relatives and am willing to admit!"

Credits:

Delaware Public Archives; Carey Family Bible; Short Family Bible; History of Delaware, Past and Present, E. Melvin Williams; The Corner Door Story

CHAPTER 9

SOME MUSINGS OF THE CAREYS
IN FRUITLAND, MARYLAND
- *MICHAEL G. (MIKE) HITCH* -

Fruitland, Maryland, or Disharoon's Crossroads as it was first called, sprang up at the confluence of several old colonial roads back just before the American Revolution in the 1760s and early 1770s. Those roads led to points north at Salisbury and on to mills at Barren Creek, Rockawalkin, Parkers mills and others up towards the Delaware line. Heading south, you had roads leading to Princess Anne and to the Pocomoke River at Dividing Creek and also down towards Wicomico Creek and the old hamlet called Upper Trappe (modern-day Allen). The Carey family made up a small group of the early settlers in the area.

At that time also, the roads that became modern-day Division Street and Meadow Bridge Road actually formed the boundary line between Somerset County to the west and Worcester County to the east – it wasn't until 1867 that Wicomico County gobbled up the entirety of Fruitland within its bounds. By then the town was named Forktown, as it had been called since the Federal Period (c1820), probably because of the forking of the roads at the current crossroads that make up Meadow Bridge Road and Division and Main Street today. It was a stopping point for stages heading north/south along the eastern shore. It was renamed Fruitland in 1873 to reflect farming practices and an abundance of crops like tomatoes and strawberries.

The land where Fruitland is located was slower to blossom because it was inland and part of a large tract called "Wicomico Manor" surveyed in 1674 for 6000 acres as a tract of "Reserves and Manors Reserved and Surveyed for His Lordship the Lord Proprietary of this Province." In other words, it was reserved for Lord Baltimore to do as he pleased – one could live there but not own the land. 6000 acres is roughly nine square miles in breadth and Wicomico Manor was laid out like a large rectangle with its length running NE to SW. The northernmost corner of the tract began where the Port Authority Building is currently located in downtown Salisbury and ran down the Wicomico (then called the Rockawalkin River) all the way to Sharps Point south of Shad Point. The line then turned inland to the southeast and ran through Fruitland to about where the modern Route 13 bypass and St. Lukes Road meet and then turns to the northeast, running to about a point at the eastern end of Schumaker Pond. The last line closes the rectangle by returning to the first point in Downtown Salisbury. As you can imagine this encompasses nearly all of where modern Fruitland now lies except for its southwest edge.

At the point where the "crossroads" was (and still is today), George Disharoon had the tract "Disharoons Adventure" surveyed for him on Mar 12 1772 for 123¼ acres described as "part in Worcester, part in Somerset, and by Disharoon's plantation." The land was rather meager as the old survey says this about it: "improvements are 120 ac of cultivated land, half under fence, other half unfenced and consists of white sandy soil, worn out." In the modern day, that tract is in the heart of the Town of Fruitland. While Disharoon never received a royal patent for his land because of the Revolution, in 1783, after the United States had won its freedom, the County Commissioners carried through the sale of all the tracts in Wicomico Manor as "Confiscated British Property" and awarded "Disharoons Adventure" to George Disharoon, for £27.12.06 (27 pounds, 12 shillings, 6 pence), citing original 1772 sale of Manor lands at £25 per 100 acres.

George Disharoon (c1741-1789) was the brother of Francis Disharoon (c1743-1788) and both were sons of John Disharoon (c1699-1761) and his wife Mary Langkake (the surname was later shortened to Lank) and grandsons of John Disharoon Sr. (1677-c1754). John Disharoon Sr. had patented the tract "Come By Chance" for 85 acres in 1713 and it borders the tract his grandson George had surveyed for him in 1772. One can see why the early name for Fruitland was "Disharoon's Crossroads"!

Many of the Carey family have lived in and around Fruitland and this writer was intrigued when he found a deed of my great grandfather Hitch from 1903 among my dad's papers for the land he was raised upon and it mentioned that it bordered Michael Carey's land. See the Figure below with a map showing some Carey land tracts in the vicinity of Fruitland, an inset of the deed mentioned and a red dot showing where this writer grew up next to Michael Carey's land. This deed caused me to do a bit more research as to who Michael Carey was.

Use the land records to help solve local history and family genealogy mysteries. The old land patents are rich with information about the land the early settlers owned and the places they lived. Old Somerset County, Maryland, was formed in 1666 and encompasses all of the area of where the modern counties of Wicomico, Worcester and Somerset in Maryland

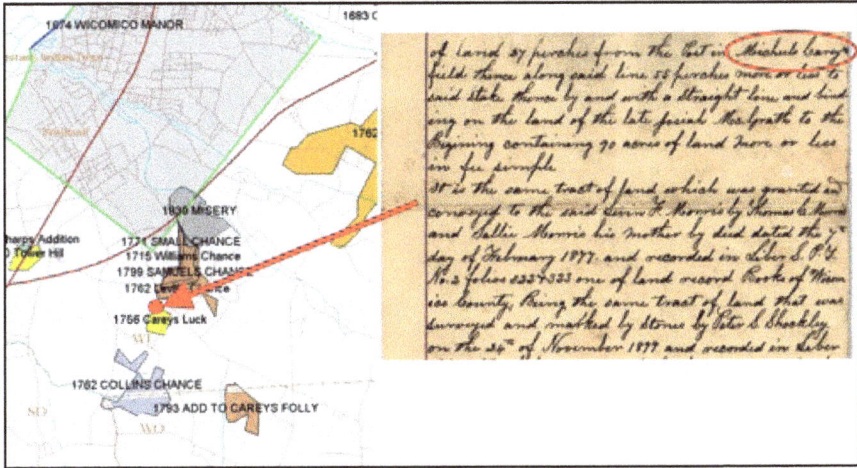

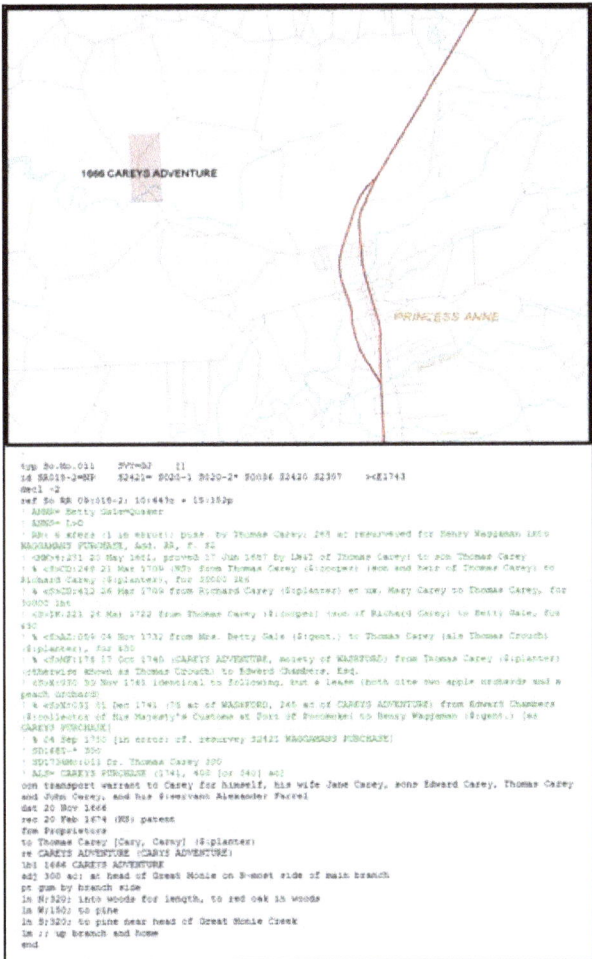

now lie and 2/3rds of modern Sussex County, Delaware. I had the pleasure of working with the late John Lyon who assembled a massive computer database of all the old land patents and other land records there that were part of Old Somerset. His work allows the researcher to quickly sort through the mountains of data there to quickly ascertain information about the early settlers and their progeny up to the time of the American Revolution.

From it, I began my quest to find out who Michael Carey was of the deed and that led me to find a nice bit of information about the Carey family who lived around the Fruitland area. This included the finding of the earliest Carey in the area, Thomas Carey, who had the 300 acre tract "Carys Adventure" surveyed for him on November 20, 1666 - he was called a "planter" in that record. It is thought that he is the earliest ancestor of all the Careys on the Delmarva Peninsula. See the Figure for a map locating where this tract was located and the computerized output that shows background of transactions involving the land up to the time of the Revolution. Note that it is northwest of Princess Anne, MD along modern day Mt. Vernon Road.

From the background information shown, we find that the settler Thomas wrote a will on May 20, 1681 that was proven June 17, 1687 that left the land to his son, Thomas Carey. Then, on March 21, 1709, the son Thomas (designated as a cooper) sold the land to Richard Carey, planter, for 30,000 pounds of tobacco. Five days later, Richard sold the land to Thomas Carey for a like amount. The land leaves the Carey family on March 26, 1722 when Richard Carey's son, Thomas, sold the land to Betty Gale for £30.

Back to my quest to find out who Michael Carey of Fruitland was. We know he descended from Thomas Carey who died sometime between 1681 and 1687, likely towards the later end of that range. Since he had land surveyed for him in 1666, he was at least age 21 at the time and probably a bit older. More research shows that Thomas Carey was named as a headright on November 14, 1653, in Lancester County, VA. It was probably he who was shown as Thomas Carey and along with 5 others was transported into that county in VA by Col. Richard Lee. That record suggests his birth year was sometime around 1633 and he came from the British Isles. His will proven in 1687 gives more clues about his family and is transcribed follows:

> *In the name of God Amen, I Thomas Cary of Great Monye in the County of Somerset and province of Maryland planter being in good health of body and of sound and perfect memory praise be therefore given to Almighty God doe make and ordain this my present last Will and testament in manner and form following, that is to say first and principally I commend my Soule into the hands of Almighty God hoping through the merits death and passion of my Savior Jesus Christ to have full and free pardon and forgiveness of all my Sins and t o inherit everlasting life , and my body I: commend it to the Earth to be decently buried at; the discretion of my Executor hereafter named and touching the disposition of all such temporal Estate as it hath pleased Almighty God to bestow upon me I give and dispose thereof as follows - First, I will that my debts and funeral charges shall be paid and discharged - Item. I give unto my son Richard Cary one hundred pounds of Tobacco - Item. I give unto my son Edward Cary one Cow yearling, Item. I give unto my son Thomas Cary after ye decease of my wife Jane Cary three hundred acres of Land*

called by the name of Caries Adventure. Item. I give unto my son John Cary a cow. Item. I give unto my son William Cary and my aforesaid son John Cary one hundred and fifty acres of Land to be equally divided between them called by the name of Washford. Item. I give unto my daughters Sarah Carey and Mary Carey one Iron gray mare and her increase. Item. I give unto my son Samuell Cary one cow - all the rest and residue of my personal Estate goods and cattle whatsoever I doe give and bequeath unto my loving wife Jane Cary and likewise all my children until they be of the age of one and twenty and her to be my full and sole executor of this my last will and testament. And I doe hereby disavow and revoke and make void all forgoing Wills and Testaments by me heretofore made. In Witness whereof I the said Thomas Cary to this my last Will and testament set my hand and seal this twentieth day of Play one thousand six hundred and Eighty one. This written will was proved by the within mentioned Dom: Copinger before me appointed by Commission. Wm. Brereton sealed John Pierce ye other witness out of the Province - Fifty acres of Land in the Forrest divided between Wm Cary and Sarah Cary, he that dyes first the other shall have it. Tomes Cary The last part of this will, a codicil, was written after the main body of the will arm would refer to fifty acres patented in 1683 by Edward Cary, in Thomas Cary's name, called Advance.

We see from here that he had eight children living at the time of his death. The one we are most interested in here is William Carey for it was his line that drifted northward from the "Carys Adventure" tract near Princess Anne to the Fruitland area. William Carey owned a lot of land during his lifetime but the tract we are most interested in for our quest for Michael Carey is "Williams Chance," a 100 acre plot William had surveyed on March 8, 1715. When William Carey's will was proven on June 19, 1734, it describes this tract as his "dwelling plantation" that he left to his son Levin Carey. The tract is located on the east side of St. Lukes Road about one mile outside the Route 13 bypass in modern day. This is near the location where this writer grew up. One further clue here was that son Levin Carey had a 50 acre plot of land surveyed for him on August 20, 1762, that bordered the south side of "William's Chance," which he named the tract "Levin's Chance." This line of Careys also later purchased adjacent lands around the area of which Michael Carey came to own.

A better illustration for the location of both of these tracts is on the first Figure mentioned previously in this chapter and, this is at the exact location referenced in my great grandfather's 1903 deed that contained "Michael Carey's field." Michael Carey (1821-1896) was the great-great-great-grandson of William Carey who died in 1734 through his son Levin Carey's (c1708-1783) line. Levin had a son William Carey (c1734-1774) who himself had a son William (c1770-1820) who had son Thomas Carey (c1794-1847) who had Michael Carey. My mystery had been solved by digging into the the old land patent records.

- Michael G. (Mike) Hitch

Chairman, Nabb Research Center Board of directors; Special Assistant to Director of NASA Space Center, Wallops, VA

Editor's Note: As indicated, Mike has found land patent records to be a valuable soure of information. He has also utilized technology to superimpose maps of original land grants on current maps. For example, he has provided land grants of the Carey's Church and Camp area, as well as other Carey family land holdings in Delmarva.

CHAPTER 10

MY LINE OF DESCENDANTS OF PETER CAREY (B. 1736)
- *R. NEILL CAREY, PhD* -

In this chapter I tell you what I know about the past few generations in my branch of the Carey family. Although I am not a genealogist, I appreciate the scholarly work that Helen Carey has done, and I eagerly read the results of her research on our ancestors. Niel reported earlier in this book that he and I discovered our common Dykes ancestry during "research time" at the Nabb Center during one of our Carey reunions; Niel's and my maternal great-great grandfather was Michael Dykes. This discovery encouraged Helen to dig deeper into our common Dykes lineage. Additionally, my mother, Pauline White Carey, was an avid genealogist, and had studied her Dykes and White ancestors. Her mother, Stella (Dykes) White, was the granddaughter of Niel's and my Michael Dykes. Fortunately, all I have to do is to soak up the wealth of information that Helen and Mom have provided. Many thanks also to my cousin Allison Carey Higgins and to my sister and brother, Jane Gardner and Sid Carey, for writing and editing with me. Writing this chapter brought back nice memories of our family and wonderful stories that I had not heard before.

Dad's first cousin, Oscar Carey, provided him with a 1992 computer printout of our Carey family tree that showed lineage back to "Thomas Cary of Monie," who reportedly came to the Maryland Colony during the 1600s (see Michael Hitch's chapter). The DNA project that Sean Gilson did with the Carey Reunion Project demonstrated that I am related to only the more recent part of that family tree, beginning with Peter Carey in the mid-1700s. Below I have listed what now seems to be our lineage, as supported by the DNA results, lifted from the Carey Family page of the Family Tree DNA website, and supplemented with family records.

- Peter Carey, born c1736, unknown wife
  - Joshua Carey c1762-1850, m. Martha Bethards in 1806 (second wife)
    - Ebenezer Carey c1818-1885, m. Henrietta Davis c1812-1870
      - Elijah Purnell Carey 1852-1927, m. Manora Toadvine 1856-c1888
        - Marion Alfred Carey 1884-1942 m. Della McGrath 1884-1978
          - Samuel Sidney Carey 1915-1994, m. Pauline White 1917-2009
            - Roger Neill Carey 1945-, Sidney Lee Carey 1949- Sara Jane (Carey) Gardner 1951-

In her chapter "My Life and Family History Research," Helen Carey mentioned the references to Peter and Joshua Carey in Samuel H. Carey's will, dated 1919. In that will, my great-grandfather, Elijah Purnell Carey (Samuel H.'s brother), received $500, Dad's father, Marion Alfred Carey, received $400 and Dad, who was 4 years old at the time, received $50.

According to a letter written in 1912 by Samuel H. Carey, he was told by his grandfather, Joshua Carey, that his great-grandfather Peter Carey came to the Whaleyville, MD, area from Petersburg, VA, in about 1773, when Joshua was about 12 years old. He stated that his father, Ebenezer Carey (my great-great-grandfather) was born when Joshua was about 60, and the family was living near Salisbury.

Information from Dad begins with his grandfather, Elijah Purnell Carey, son of Ebenezer Carey. Elijah Purnell was a farmer who lived East of Salisbury, in an area near Powellville known as Shavox. Sometime around 1900 he moved his family to a farm on Mt. Hermon Rd., near Carey Ave., just East of Salisbury. Dad remembered taking walks with him at family get-togethers. Dad's grandmother, Manora Toadvine Carey, died when my grandfather, Marion Carey, was about 4 years old. I don't remember hearing about her from Dad, except that she was buried in a plot that Marion could no longer find when he took Dad to look for her grave. After Manora died, Elijah Purnell married Manora's sister Cora Toadvine, who raised Manora's three children, and had three of her own children with Elijah Purnell. Dad spoke affectionately of Aunt Cora. Elijah Purnell, Cora, and some of the children are buried in Parsons Cemetery in Salisbury. Here is a picture of the family taken on the porch of their farm house on Mt. Hermon Rd., near Carey Ave. Manora's sons Emory, Marion, and Elihu, are standing with Elijah Purnell and Aunt Cora between them (Marion and Elihu). Seated are Cora's children Ethel, Oscar, and Ralph. All received inheritances in Samuel H. Carey's will.

Dad's father Marion Alfred Carey, was born in 1884. He married Della McGrath of Crisfield. Marion had several businesses. He had a farm on Backbone Rd. in Eden in Somerset County. Dad remembered that his father did not buy a truck for the farm, but used a large open car instead. At different times he also had a livery stable, a dairy, and the Salisbury Hotel, which was on Railroad Ave. Dad's parents were living on Wailes St. in Salisbury when Dad was born in 1915. An older sister, Manora, had died before Dad was born. After Dad, came Sara Jane (born 1917) and Alfred Walton (born 1923). The family moved to the hotel when the children were fairly young. The family are pictured here on the back steps of the hotel when Alfred was an infant. Dad's room was at the top of the stairs in the hotel.

Grandmother Carey worked hard to keep the hotel going when Grandfather was tied up with the other businesses. In those days, salesmen ("drummers") would come to town on the train, and stay at the hotel for a few days while they made rounds in the area in a rented rig. Grandmother and her crew would make meals for the hotel's guests and pack lunches for them. Grandmother had been trained as a milliner (hat-maker), and was an excellent seamstress. In spite of their hard work,

the Depression ruined them. They lost nearly everything. The hotel burned in the early 1940s, shortly after they lost it.

Like other children of the Depression, Dad struggled to get an education. He did an extra year at high school to get "business" training, which was then typing, stenography, and bookkeeping. He taught Business at Crisfield High School for some weeks, substituting when his uncle Joseph McGrath was ill. He enrolled at Salisbury Teachers' College, working various part-time jobs, including at Hayman's Drug Store on East Main St. He was in the first four-year class, graduating in 1937 with a degree in Elementary Education.

Dad taught for a couple of years in Sparks, MD, but teaching was not for him. He returned to Salisbury in 1939, and took a job as part-time announcer and part-time janitor at WSAL radio. The studio was on East Main St. During this period, Dad was involved in local amateur theater in a group that became the Community Players. Dad had a tonsillectomy shortly after his return to Salisbury and was in Peninsula General Hospital when he met Mom, Pauline White, who was his nurse. Mom had hopes of being a school teacher, but went to nurses' school because it was more affordable. Her parents, Martin and Stella White, had a farm at the corner of Meadow Bridge and Backbone Rds., a few miles southeast of Fruitland, MD.

WSAL lost their license in 1940. A new station, WBOC, would go on the air later that year, and they had a position for Dad, but he needed to find something else to do for a few months. Dad took a job with John A. Price, a produce buyer and wholesaler. Sometimes Dad would bid on produce as farmers came through the Auction Block. Mom's Dad told her about a strange occurrence one day when his watermelons were bid up higher than the other farmers' watermelons.

Dad went to WBOC as an announcer when it went on the air in 1940. Sometimes he had to work on Mom's day off, and she would come to the radio station with him and listen to recordings of radio shows while he was on the air. They were married on Thanksgiving Day that year and honeymooned on the Skyline Drive. In 1942 they moved to Richmond, where Dad took a job with WRVA Radio. WRVA was a "clear channel" station, meaning that, at night, WRVA, with its high-power transmitter, could broadcast their signal into a wide listening area. Dad spoke of receiving letters from listeners from as far away as the Dakotas. This was the Golden Age of radio, and Dad had many great experiences. One of his announcing gigs was as the "Funny Money Man." It was wartime, and we have pictures of him interviewing Tyrone Power during a War Bonds drive, doing live announcing as a warship is launched in Norfolk, and doing other remote broadcasts. WRVA's studios and offices were in the Hotel Richmond, right across from Capital Square. At WRVA Dad produced "The Old Dominion Barn Dance," at the Lyric Theater, also across the street from the hotel. The house band was John and Mary Workman's band, called "Sunshine Sue and her Rangers." The Old Dominion Barn Dance and Sunshine Sue had a great run. The Barn Dance was broadcast nationally on CBS and Armed Forces Radio. In producing the Barn Dance Dad worked with a variety of country music stars, including Minnie Pearl, Granpa Jones, Mother Maybelle and the Carter Sisters, and Chet Adkins.

Dad had a great voice and spoke well. People still tell me how much they liked to listen to him speak.

Mom was a Public Health Nurse when they first moved to

Richmond, and then became an instructor in Nursing Arts in the Nursing Program at Grace Hospital. Dad had a bleeding ulcer that would take him near death on several occasions. The drugs that people take routinely now to prevent ulcers didn't exist then, and gastric ulcer was a significant cause of death. The treatment was a lengthy rest in a hospital with buffering solutions dripped into the patient's stomach through a naso-gastric tube. Dad hemorrhaged badly when Mom was due to have me, and he wound up in Grace Hospital for an extended period. Mom's OB doctor was a professor at Medical College of Virginia, but he could not deliver me at Grace. So, Mom had to find another doctor. The nurses recommended Dr. Homer Ferguson, the OB doctor at Grace. He delivered me, and I turned out OK, in spite of coming out feet first, with the cord wrapped around my neck. Mom and I were lucky to survive it. (The Fergusons became family friends, and he delivered my brother and sister, too.) Within a day or so of my birth, Mom's supervisor fixed it up so Mom and Dad and I had our own room in the hospital.

My brother Sidney Lee was born in January 1949. When he was still an infant, Dad went to Lahey Clinic in Boston for surgery on his ulcer. Dad's doctor was concerned that Dad would die if he had another big hemorrhage. In fact, Dad was hemorrhaging when he got to Lahey, and they took him right to the OR. The surgery was transformative. Dad went from los-ing several weeks a year due to his ulcer and being chronically anemic, to being in good health. Projects that were on hold got completed. One was a HiFi that Dad built from scratch out of mahogany. Previously Dad would work on it for a while, then get sickand have to put the parts under the bed, and then get back to it when he felt better. Dad was a craftsman, and the hi-fi turned out beautifully. We still listen to it.

Dad's good health enabled him and Mom to think about building a house. They still didn't have much money after Dad's years of illness, but their friends Ralph and Muriel Roberts had money to buy two adjacent lots in Henrico County, near Richmond. In return, Dad was the general contractor for houses for the Roberts and us. They were mirror images of each other. This was 1951, during the Korean War, and there were shortages of building materials, so Dad had to be on the lookout for the time when distributors had things like water heaters available. We moved into our new house in September, 1951 just before my sister Sara Jane was born. The houses turned out beautifully, and the Roberts were lifelong friends.

In 1957 WRVA-TV Channel 12 went on the air in Richmond with Dad as Program Director. At one point their network was ABC-Mutual, which at the time did not have a full schedule of shows. So WRVA-TV built up a large library of movies to show during the network's quiet periods. Dad made sure he saw every movie that went on the air. When we came to visit Grandfather and Grandmother White in Salisbury, he would bring a projector and several films so he could preview movies. He would hang a sheet on the wall, and project onto it. Grandad loved the Westerns and there were plenty of them. Soon WRVA-TV became an NBC affiliate, in part because of the pitch Dad made to the network executives in New York. We have a memo from his boss thanking him for his great job in that effort.

Mom and Dad always said they wanted to get back to the Eastern Shore someday, and that day finally came in 1969 when WRVA was sold, and Dad came to Salisbury to manage WBOC radio and television. Mom had taken a nursing refresher course in Richmond and went back to work in the Wicomico Public Health Department in the psychiatric clinic. According to coworkers and ex-patients, she was really good at it. Occasionally, when I was out with her, former patients would see her and thank her for helping them.

Dad had a good run at WBOC. When the radio and television stations were being sold and had to be split up due to an FCC regulation at the time, he went with the radio stations to finish his career. He retired in the early 1980s but was called out of retirement later to manage them for a couple of years after his successor did not work out.

Dad and Mom had a wonderful retirement. They built a "cottage" on Deal Island in the mid-1970s and lived there in the summers, commuting to Salisbury while they were still working. It was the center of their lives and of family activities during the season. They hosted several family reunions there. Our nieces and nephews from the Midwest have fond memories of visits to Deal Island and fishing and crabbing with Dad and then cooking up the catch with Mom. Dad died in 1994, and Mom died in 2009.

Dad's sister, Aunt Sara, worked for the telephone company for her entire career, starting in Salisbury, working part-time when she was in school, and eventually holding supervisory positions in Laurel, MD and Havre de Grace, MD. She married Richard B. Eaton (born 1900) in 1951. Uncle Dick was a railway postal clerk and sorted mail on the Washington, DC to Pittsburgh, PA run for many years. They did not have children, but were very good to us nieces and nephews. Uncle Dick died in 1990 and Aunt Sara died in 2010.

Dad's brother, Uncle Al, served in the Army in the Philippines, New Guinea, and Australia in WWII. On his return he was trained in gasoline pump maintenance under the GI bill with our Great Uncle Morris McGrath in Menlo Park, NJ. While he was working with Uncle Mac, the owner of Al's favorite luncheonette introduced him to Jeanette Larsen (born 1923) who worked at Commonwealth Bank in Metuchen, NJ. They hit it off, and were married in 1950. Al adopted her young son from a previous marriage, Roy, who considered Al to be his father. Roy was a real cousin to us. Al and Jeanette celebrated the birth of their daughter Allison in 1954.

Al stayed in New Jersey and spent most of his career working for an automotive parts distributor, Summit Motor Parts, selling to auto dealerships and body shops. He represented all of the large US auto makers. When the dealers and manufacturers were clearing space of old parts stock to make room for parts for newer models, he saw an opportunity, and bought up the "new" old stock, saving it from scrappers, and selling it instead to antique automobile restorers. His business, "LAS Chance Ford Parts," became the largest distributor in the Eastern US, concentrating on Ford, Lincoln and Mercury parts. Al worked many of the large swap meets, handled walk-ins at his warehouse and shop, and had a huge mail order business. This was before the days of personal computers and the Internet. Al had a few antique cars himself, including his custom-made antique milk truck and others that were in the movies, i.e., The Godfather and The Valachi Papers. Al served as Worshipful Master Mason of Masonic Lodge #135 in Metuchen, NJ.

Like Dad, Uncle Al had a bleeding ulcer. In one episode the doctors went through 30 pints of his blood type (relatively rare O-negative) and 2 pints of plasma to save his life. Several of his Masonic Lodge brothers and Aunt Jeanette's cousin,

Vivian Serko, drove to New York City Hospitals to obtain additional blood during a record-setting snowstorm that dumped over a foot of snow on NYC. During surgery his stomach ruptured and was partially removed. He wore an abdominal support brace for the rest of his life. Doctors did not perform any further surgeries on him in fear of excessive bleeding.

After Roy and Allison were older Jeanette was as secretary for Edison, NJ Board of Education from 1968 to 1986. Following retirement she worked as part time secretary for the Roth Insurance Agency in Waretown, NJ, and bookkeeper for LAS Chance Auto Parts. She was known for her excellent needlework, and she created family fashions, complex home furnishings and décor, and theatrical costumes for students in the schools where she worked. She created many dresses for children's charities and Barbie fashions, which were donated to and sold by local charities. She knitted and crocheted baby sweater, hat and bootie sets, afghans for the old, young, tall and short, darned socks, tatted doilies and needle-pointed chair cushions. Uncle Al died in 1983 and Aunt Jeanette died in 1993.

Roy was in service as a radioman and microwave repairman in the US Army Signal Corps in Da Nang, Viet Nam, at the time of the Tet Offensive in 1968. When he returned home he attended Middlesex County College and earned his degree in Electronics Technology and later attended Monmouth College in Long Branch, NJ, on the GI Bill. Roy worked as Research and Development Engineer, Network Systems Information Technology Specialist for Bell Telephone Laboratories (AT&T) at Holmdel, NJ. Roy was an amateur radio operator, surf fisherman, bicyclist, sailor, and musician. He played trombone, marimba, guitar and banjo. He was a founding member of Vietnam Veterans of America Chapter 12 in Ocean Township, NJ, and was active in Vietnam Veteran organizations and activities.

Roy married his high school sweetheart Sheila Elizabeth Varga (born 1948) in 1970. Sheila, a Registered Nurse, received her training at Beth Israel School of Nursing, NYC, and worked as an OR Nurse at Memorial Sloan Kettering Cancer Center in NYC. Their daughter Samantha Ann was born in 1974 and son Elijah Aaron, in 1980. Roy and Sheila loved to dance. Roy died in 2012.

Samantha is a graduate of Moore College of Art and Design, Philadelphia, PA, BFA Fashion Design. She is married, and has two children. Samantha creates unique jewelry which she markets on Etsy.

Elijah attended Marywood University, Scranton, PA then received his BS in Internet Marketing from Full Sail University, Winter Park, FL and MBA in Marketing Research and Analytics from Southern New Hampshire University, Manchester, NH. Elijah is a creative self-taught artist with over 500 paintings of various styles, mediums, sizes and subjects on display in residential and commercial spaces worldwide. Selected artwork and artist quotes from Elijah have been published in these award-winning book titles "The Art of Everyday Joe: A Collector's Journal", "Art In King Size Beds: A Collector's Journal", and "Art For The People: A Collector's Journal" by Michael K. Corbin.

Allison has wonderful stories about growing up with Uncle Al and Aunt Jeanette and Roy, including this one:

> "We all ate dinner at the kitchen table at six o'clock when Dad came home from work. He had food allergies. Mom had gall bladder trouble.

Mom's father Grandpop Larsen couldn't have salt. Grandma Larsen liked peace and quiet. We never had fried food unless Dad made eggs fried in bacon grease or Grandma Carey made fried chicken for Dad when she was staying with us. We ate grilled, broiled, or steamed. I found out about garlic from our Italian neighbors only by chance. They would bring us left-over home-made pasta and Roy would intercept every bowl at the front door. It wasn't until he was in Vietnam that I got to try some. Delicious! He did the same thing with the jars of figs Grandma Carey's sisters would send up to us each year. He told me they tasted nasty and I believed him. More for him. We laughed about it as adults."

Allison attended colleges in New Jersey. She worked for 30 years as a financial analyst and reinsurance recovery specialist for several large reinsurance companies, collecting balances owed from insurance companies, both domestic and foreign, for amounts due from large losses such as environmental (for example, asbestos) and property damage (such as hurricane losses). Her job gave her travel opportunities too.

She met her future husband Brian Higgins when her boss asked her to give a ride to her daughter's boyfriend who was an operator in the computer room. They became friends because of common interests in the beach and live music. Brian spent most of his professional career as a computer network technician based out of Edison, NJ for Wakefern Food Corporation, the parent company of ShopRite, and he was on call 24/7 for nearly 25 years. Brian knew everybody in the Jersey Beach music scene, and over the years he has managed bands, been on cable TV and radio, and even recorded demo tapes in their kitchen in the days before home PC recording equipment became affordable. Allison tells of coming home from her corporate job to find Rock and Roll Hall of Famers sitting on the couch waiting to pick up live recordings. They have participated in many music festivals, including Pete Seeger's Clearwater Fest. The music took them across the country and overseas, and they hosted many musicians and fans in their home over the years.

When the terrorist attack on the World Trade Center Twin Towers took place in 2001, Allison was working for an insurance company that reported to a division in the Towers, and also worked with independent brokers and intermediaries who had offices in the towers. She lost many friends and colleagues; everyone in her community in New Jersey knew someone who was lost.

Brian and Allison are members of The Asbury Ushers, a group of volunteers. They have ushered parades, beer, oyster, and music festivals, public dedications, Monmouth University football games, the Bruce Springsteen Symposium, the Beatles Symposium, charity events and dance recitals. They have hosted The Price is Right, Thomas the Train, So You Think You Can Dance, The New Jersey Hall of Fame Inductions and the Bruce on Broadway rehearsals. They volunteer for local musical foundations. Like Al, they have an antique car, a 1961 Mercury Comet in original condition with mint green paint, a crowd favorite and award winner.

As far back as I can remember, we met Uncle Al's family at Aunt Sara and Uncle Dick's home in Havre de Grace for Thanksgiving. Grandmother Carey (Della) split the year among us, the Eatons and the New Jersey Careys, and she usually made the move during those meetings. We have kept the tradition alive, and still meet the New Jersey cousins in Havre de Grace at Thanksgiving to catch up.

My sister Jane, and brother Sid, and I were raised in Richmond.

I was trained as an analytical chemist at the University of Richmond and Duke University, and worked as a Clinical Chemist in the Laboratory of the University of Wisconsin Hospital in Madison, WI, and at Peninsula Regional Medical Center here in Salisbury. The collaborative relationships developed during my time at the University of Wisconsin stayed with me throughout my career, and opened many doors for me. I am retired, but still consult a day or so a week. I met Nancy Temperly (born 1944), a medical technologist and laboratory supervisor at the University of Wisconsin, and we were married in 1977. We have lived in Salisbury since moving here in 1977. Coincidentally, we live in the Newtown Historic District Victorian neighborhood of Salisbury, about 4 blocks west of the location of the Salisbury Hotel that was owned and operated by my grandparents, Marion and Della Carey. We have no children.

I learned to sail on the lakes in Madison and have raced a sailboat on the Nanticoke River for many years. Radio runs in our family; I am an amateur radio operator, mostly working in Morse code. Nancy has volunteered in several nonprofit organizations since we have been married, and she and I stay active in neighborhood and civic activities. Her family were dairy farmers near Galena, IL. We enjoy visiting her three sisters who still live in the Galena area.

Sid received a business degree from Lambuth College in Jackson, Tennessee, where he was manager of the college radio station. Sid spent his working career with the Internal

Revenue Service in Tennessee. He started as an auditor, and then served as manager in several departments at different levels in the IRS, in Jackson, Nashville, and Memphis. Sid is a master at restoring antique automobiles and has been active in antique automobile clubs and events for most of his adult life. When he married Donna Tapper (1950) in Memphis in 1984, Jane and I rode in the wedding procession in the rumble seat of a 1934 Ford. Sid has won best of show several times over the years with different cars he has restored. Jane and I have done several antique car tours with Sid. Sid and Donna live in the Memphis, TN, area. She also had a long career with IRS, as an agent in Memphis. Donna is a master gardener. Donna's daughter from her first marriage, Lisa Childers, was born in 1976 and died in 2012.

Jane received her degree in English from the University of Maryland and followed Dad into the broadcast industry, even working two summers at WBOC in Salisbury. For more than twenty years, Jane covered the medical beat in Norfolk, VA. Her work took her all over the nation and the world, reporting on the beginning of the AIDS crisis, ground-breaking work in surgery to correct facial deformities with the charity Operation Smile, and the literal birth of in vitro fertilization in America with the birth of "test-tube baby" Elizabeth Jordan Carr in Norfolk.

She finished her television career as news anchor at WTKR-TV in Norfolk before working in public relations at Eastern Virginia Medical School. She was inducted into the Virginia Communications Hall of Fame in 2018. Jane married a fellow University of Maryland Terp, Gary Gardner (born 1947), in 1973. At the beginning of his career, Gary was a radio announcer and production manager in several stations in

Maryland and Virginia. Later he went back to school to get his Master's in Teaching and taught English in Virginia Beach for many years. He still enjoys substitute teaching there. For many years Jane and Gary had a "cottage" in Duck, NC, and hosted family get-togethers. They now live in downtown Norfolk next to the slip in which the battleship Wisconsin is berthed.

- R. Neill Carey

Editor's note: Neill and Nancy Carey have been active, enthusiastic members of the Carey/Cary Family organization, attending and presenting at Carey/Cary Family reunions. Their interest and active involvement in historic parts of the Salisbury area complements their interest in family history.

CHAPTER II

THE BALTIMORE CAREYS

- ANTHONY MORRIS (TONY) CAREY III -

John Carey was the first member of the Carey family to live in Baltimore. He was born in 1707 and died in 1763. With his wife Aberilla, he had a home on Gwynn's Falls below the Frederick Road, and he owned a piece of property in Baltimore County called "Little Munster." John was a farmer and a hammerman, a job associated with the mining of ore. He served as a vestryman at Old St. Paul's Church and is buried in its nearby cemetery in Baltimore City. John and Aberilla had four children: daughters Eleanor and Margaret and twin sons, John and James.

Eleanor married Colonel Cristopher Randall, whose descendants included James R. Randall, author of the State song, "Maryland My Maryland." Margaret married John Martin, employed in 1776 by the State of Maryland as the captain of a ship transporting supplies from Martinique to Annapolis.

Little is known about son John who died unmarried, but John's twin brother James was in the shipping and milling businesses and became one of the principal financiers of Baltimore. When the Revolutionary War began, he was in England where he was detained until the war ended. On his return in 1790 he helped organize the Bank of Maryland of which he later became President and served as a director of the Bank of America, an insurance company and several road and turnpike companies. He partnered with Tench Tilghman, a former officer and aide-de-camp to George Washington in a business shipping hogsheads of tobacco to France. When Baltimore became a City in 1797, he was elected to the first City Council and served on it intermittently until 1815.

James owned a country estate called Loudon Park in West Baltimore, now the Loudon Park Cemetery where he, his wife and a number of relatives are buried. James is usually referred to as James Carey of Loudon to distinguish him from later James Careys in the family.

He was originally an Episcopalian, but in 1785 married Martha Ellicott, a member of a mill owning family in Howard County and converted to the Quaker faith, an event that had a determining effect on his life and that of his descendants. The wedding took place on horseback at the old Friends Meeting House at Elkridge Landing where ceremonies were often performed on horseback, since carriages could rarely be used due to the poor condition of the roads.

In his later years James Carey devoted much of his activities to improving the lot of African Americans. He was the Vice-Chairman of the Maryland Abolition Society. In 1802 at a time when African Americans could not legally own property, James Carey conveyed land to Quaker trustees for the Sharp Street Methodist Church and School, one of the oldest black churches in Baltimore City still active today. Carey Street in West Baltimore is named after him.

James and Martha had three daughters: Hannah, Margaret and Martha and three sons: John Ellicott, Samuel and George:

Hannah married William E. Coale at a Friends meeting house in 1823. Margaret was the wife of Galloway Cheston, the first President of the Board of Trustees of Hopkins University. Martha married Dr. Richard Henry Thomas, a practicing physician in Baltimore and professor of obstetrics and medical jurisprudence at the University of Maryland. They had three sons: two died shortly after birth; the third, Dr. James Carey Thomas, born in 1833, married Mary Whitall from a Philadelphia Quaker family. He practiced medicine in Baltimore and was a member of the first Board of Trustees of Johns Hopkins University and Bryn Mawr College. He served as President of the YMCA and was a prominent member of the Orthodox Friends who worshipped at the meeting house at Eutaw and Monument Street in Baltimore. His wife Mary Whitall Thomas, also an eminent member of the Society of Friends, was a founder of the YWCA, an active member of the Women's Christian Temperance Union and Vice President of the Baltimore Orphan Asylum.

James and Mary Thomas were the parents of ten children, eight of whom grew to adulthood: Martha Carey, John M. Whitall, Henry M., Bond Valentine, Mary Grace, Margaret Cheston, Helen and Frank Snowden.

Martha Carey Thomas, a prominent educator known as M. Carey Thomas, lived from 1857 to 1935. She was one of the five founders of Bryn Mawr School in Baltimore and the second President of Bryn Mawr College. From an early age she exhibited an independence of mind and drive to succeed. After graduating from Cornell University, she wanted to go to Hopkins University for a graduate degree, but even though her father and other male Quakers were members of the Board of Trustees, it was ruled she would be allowed to attend only as an auditor sitting behind a curtain so as not to distract the male students. Finding that arrangement unsatisfactory, she went to Europe and earned her PhD in philology summa cum laude from the University of Zurich.

And she got her revenge on Hopkins. When Johns Hopkins died, he set up a trust for the University and the Hospital but did not provide enough funds to build a medical school. M. Carey Thomas, along with four close female friends, the wealthiest being Mary Garrett, daughter of the founder of the B&O railroad, raised $100,000 for the construction of the medical school provided it would admit women. The Trustees then said the project would cost $500,000. With Mary Garrett putting up $307,000 more, and M. Carey Thomas taking the lead in negotiating with the Trustees, the Johns Hopkins School of Medicine was established, becoming one of the first medical schools in the country to admit women.

With respect to the three sons of James Carey and Martha Ellicott, Samuel, the oldest, married Martha Evans of Buffalo, New York, but was not active in business. George, the youngest, born in 1800, married Mary Gibson of Richmond Virginia, and was later President of the Peabody Fire Company of Baltimore, a position he held until his death in 1865. Their oldest son, James, served in the Confederate Army until the end of the Civil War. Their second son, George Gibson Carey married Josephine Clemm Poe, daughter of Judge Nielson Poe, and became the headmaster of a secondary school in Baltimore. Known initially as the Carey School, it became the Boys' Latin School and exists today.

George and Josephine Carey were the parents of three surviving daughters: Josephine Gibson, Maria Gibson and Margaret Cheston and two sons: George Gibson, Jr. and Nielson Poe.

Josephine Gibson Carey married Dr. Henry Thomas, the son of Dr. James Carey and Mary Whitall Thomas, the first

Clinical Professor of Neurology at Johns Hopkins Medical School and served actively in that capacity for 30 years. Josephine and Henry were the parents of Dr. Henry M. Thomas Jr. and Edward Trudeau Thomas.

Dr. Henry M. Thomas Jr. who died in 1966 was a practicing physician, member of the Hopkins Medical School faculty and co-founder of the Thyroid Clinic at Hopkins. He married Caroline C. Bedell, a distinguished research physician at Johns Hopkins Medical School who forged new pathways in preventative medicine. They were the parents of Dr. Henry M. Thomas III, Eleanor Carey Thomas and Mary Whitall Thomas. Dr. Henry M. Thomas III specialized in pulmonology and married Karen Ann Purin, and they have two children: Sarah Whitall Thomas and Richard Loos Thomas. Mary Whitall Thomas married William Murrie Clevenger and they have three children: James Thomas Clevenger, Caroline Murrie Clevenger and Andrew Whitall.

Edward Trudeau Thomas was born in Baltimore and died in 1973 in Princeton New Jersey. In 1925, he studied as a Rhodes Scholar at Oxford University. He was the headmaster of several private schools, was a naval officer during World War II and after the war the dean of admissions at Hofstra University. He married Martha Botsford and they had three children: James Carey Thomas, Henry Botsford Thomas and Patricia Carey Thomas.

George Gibson Carey, Jr. married S. Rosalie MacGill. The couple lived in Riderwood, a suburban area of Baltimore County where tragically Mrs. Carey was killed by a train while crossing the tracks at the Riderwood station. George and Rosalie were the parents of George G. Carey III, Margaret Cheston Carey, Constance MacGill Carey and Josephine Fitzgerald (Zoe)

Carey. George Gibson Carey III married Margaret Hambleton and they were the parents of George Gibson Carey IV.

George Gibson (Gibby) Carey IV graduated from Gilman School and Princeton University and married Anna Kirwin (AK) Steck of Baltimore. The couple lived in Cincinnati, Ohio, where he served as the Vice-President for Marketing of the Procter & Gamble Company. After retiring, he and his wife maintained a farm outside the City. They are the parents of Margaret Elliott Carey, who married David DeMichellis; George Gibson Carey V, husband of Hampton Daniel; Frederick Riddick Carey, who married Deena Jacobs; and Eugenia (Jenny) Carey, wife of Patrick Randolph.

John Ellicott Carey, the second son of James Carey and Martha Ellicott, married Ann Head Irwin of Alexandria, Virginia and was involved in the export of flour. He and his wife were the parents of two sons: James and Thomas. James, later known as James Carey of the Mount, was born in 1821 and died in 1894 at the Mount, the family estate in the Walbrook section of West Baltimore. The 10,000 square foot building at the Mount is a large Italianate structure designed by William Reasin, a well-known local architect. After James' death, it was sold and for some time occupied by a non-profit organization that provided support services for persons with developmental disabilities. Recently it has been unoccupied.

James of the Mount graduated from Haverford College and married Susan Kimber from a Philadelphia Quaker family. He was in business for many years in Baltimore City, a director of the Union Bank and Central Savings Bank, trustee of John Hopkins Hospital, first president of the Provident Savings Bank, and an elder in the Orthodox Society of Friends. James and Susan were the parents of six children: Thomas Kimber,

James Carey of the Mount

John Ellicott, James, Mary Irwin, Francis King and Anthony Morris.

Thomas Kimber Carey lived on Park Avenue in Baltimore and married Mary King, daughter of Francis T. King, a Baltimore merchant who helped Quaker philanthropist Johns Hopkins establish the hospital and university in Baltimore. Mary King was an organizer of the Young Women's Christian Association and its President at the time of her death in 1908. In 1886 Thomas founded Thomas K. Carey & Brothers, which subsequently became Carey Machinery and Supply Company described below. At the time of his death in 1847 he was a director of the Merchants National Bank and the Baltimore Equitable Society.

John Ellicott Carey married Susannah Murdock of Claiborne County, Mississippi, attended Haverford College, was a founder and supporter of the Baltimore Cricket Club and had a national reputation as a cricketer. A cotton goods merchant, he represented cotton mills throughout the South. He died in 1934.

James Carey, third son of James Carey of the Mount and Susan Carey, lived in Baltimore and died in 1939. He married Anna King, daughter of Francis T. King, and subsequently Caroline Maccoun. A graduate of Haverford College and the University of Maryland Law School, in 1885 James with his brother Francis King Carey, published Carey's Forms and Precedents, which at the time of his death was still used throughout the State. He served as Trustee Chairman of the Homewood

Friends Meeting and was an active member of the Miles White Beneficial Society of Baltimore City, a charitable trust affiliated with the Baltimore Quaker Yearly Meeting.

Mary Irwin Carey married Francis Greenleaf Allison of Providence, Rhode Island, a professor at Brown University. The couple had two children: Susanna and Henry.

Francis King Carey who lived from 1858 to 1944 attended Haverford College and the University of Maryland Law School. He was a prominent lawyer in Baltimore and a founding member of two well-known Baltimore law firms: Steele, Semmes and Carey, later Semmes, Bowen and Semmes, and Carey, Piper and Hall, which eventually became DLA Piper. He served as President of the Charleston Consolidated Railway, Gas and Electric Company and later as Chairman of the Board of the National Sugar Manufacturing Company, helped to save the sugar beet industry from collapse. After the great Baltimore fire of 1904, he was appointed to the Mayor's Executive Municipal Corporation charged with planning the rebuilding of the burned areas and was influential in persuading the Baltimore business community to finance many needed but costly infrastructure improvements. He married Anne Galbraith Hall who was instrumental in establishing the private Gilman School in Baltimore that has been attended by a number of Careys and relatives. Francis and Anne were the parents of Louise, Francis James, Margaret, Eleanor, Andrew, and Reginald.

Louise married Joshua Rosett, a physician, and died in New York in 1975. Francis James Carey was born in 1888 and died in 1949. He went to Gilman School and Harvard College and served with the American Expeditionary Force in France and Germany during World War I. A graduate of the University of Maryland Law School, he compiled a book on Maryland Corporation Law with McKenzie Edgerton. He was a legal adviser to the Potomac Edison Company for thirty years, succeeding his father Francis King Carey in that position. He had two sons with Marjorie Aylesford Armstrong of Wilmington, North Carolina: Francis James Carey, Jr., and William Polk Carey.

Margaret Townsend Carey, the second daughter of Francis and Anne Carey married Percy Childs Madeira, Jr., of Philadelphia, Pennsylvania, in 1914. A Captain in World War I, Mr. Madeira was the Vice President of the coal operators Madeira Hill & Company, a Trustee of the Pennsylvania Society of the Deaf and Dumb and a fellow of the Royal Geographic Society. Margaret and Percy were the parents of Eleanor Irwin Carey, Percy Childs III, and Francis King Carey Madeira who married Jean R. Browning. After studying piano at the Julliard School in New York, Francis Madeira was an associate professor of music at Brown University and founded the Rhode Island Philharmonic Orchestra.

Andrew Galbraith Carey, son of Francis King and Anne Galbraith Carey, was born in 1899 and died in 1974. He went to Gilman School and graduated from Princeton. A vice president and director of Carey Machinery & Supply Company, during World War II he served in the Navy and at various times was attached to the Office of War Mobilization and the Office of Strategic Services. He was married first to Lorna Underwood and second to Dr. Jane Perry Clark, a political science professor at Columbia University with whom he co-authored a book *The Web of Modern Greek Politics*. Andrew and Lorna Carey were the parents of Lorna Underwood who married John O. Mack of Concord, Massachusetts, and Andrew Galbraith (Drew) Carey.

Drew Carey attended Gilman School, graduated from

Princeton and earned a PhD from Yale University. He is a former Professor of Ocean Ecology and Biogeochemistry at the College of Earth, Ocean and Atmospheric Sciences of Oregon State University. He married Elizabeth van Kleek Menges who died in 2000 and then Alison Fletcher Walker. Drew and Elizabeth were the parents of Todd Loring Carey and Arianne van Kleek Carey. He and his wife Alison live in Chatham, Massachusetts.

Reginald Shober Carey, the third son of Francis King and Anne Galbraith Carey was born in 1906 and died in 1975. Like many relatives, he went to Gilman School and Princeton University and also attended classes at the University of Grenoble and Oxford. He was in the foreign service and appointed a Vice-Consul in Berlin in 1932 but resigned to work for the family's National Sugar Manufacturing Company in Sugar City, Colorado. He married Margaretta Bayard Wright and the couple were the parents of: Elise, J. Bayard of Port Richmond, California, Reginald S. Jr. who died in infancy, and Francis King Carey 2nd, one of 39 officers and men lost in the sinking of the nuclear submarine Scorpion.

Francis James Carey Jr. the older son of Francis James Carey and Marjorie Armstrong was born in 1926 and died in 2014. A naval officer during World War II, he graduated from the University of Pennsylvania and its Law School. He was a partner in the law firm of Reed Smith LLP and served as President of W.P. Carey & Company founded by his brother, William Polk Carey. He had two children by his first wife, Mary Crozier Page: Francis J. Carey III and Elizabeth Carey, and by a second marriage to Emily Norris Large, three children: H. Augustus Carey, Emily Norris Carey and Francis W. Carey.

William Polk (Bill) Carey, the younger son of Francis

William P. Carey

James Carey and Marjorie Armstrong, was born in 1930 and died in 2012. He attended Calvert and Gilman chools in Baltimore, the Pomfret School in Connecticut, Princeton University which he left supposedly for not compiling a sufficient number of chapel credits, then graduated from the Wharton Business School at the University of Pennsylvania. He worked for his stepfather's car dealership in New Jersey where he learned the lease financing business that he used subsequently to establish W. P. Carey, Inc., in 1973, a real estate investment trust engaged in the sale and leaseback financing of properties in the United States and abroad. The firm's stock is listed on the New York Stock Exchange.

Bill was an active philanthropist and made a number of generous gifts through the W.P. Carey Foundation to Baltimore institutions, including substantial donations to Johns Hopkins University for the Carey Business School named for his great-great-great grandfather, James Carey of Loudon; to the University of Maryland School of Law named for his grandfather, Francis King Carey; and to Arizona State University for its business school named after him. His Foundation made gifts to Calvert School in Baltimore for a new middle school named the Francis J. Carey Hall for his brother and for the W.P. Carey Lower School in honor of the School's most generous alumni donor. Bill's Foundation also made a substantial contribution to facilitate the acquisition of the former Alex Brown family building and its interconnection to the adjacent Baltimore School for the Arts building in Mount Vernon Place. The former Alex Brown building is named the Anthony M. Carey III building in honor of his second cousin, the founding Chairman of the School's Board of Trustees.

In 2006 the Foundation provided funds to Gilman School for the renovation of the School's main building named Carey Hall after Bill's grandmother, Anne Galbraith Carey, who with assistance of her husband, Francis King Carey and Dr. Daniel Coit Gilman, the first president of Johns Hopkins University, established the School. Recently the Foundation made a gift to the Maryland Historical Society to endow the Carey Center for Maryland Life to highlight the family contributions to the civic, educational, legal and economic life of the State dating back to the 18th century.

Anthony Morris Carey, the youngest son of James Carey of the Mount and Susan Kimber, who used the first name Morris, was born on January 11, 1861, at the Mount and died on May 14, 1938, survived by his wife, Margaret Thomas Carey and five children: G. Cheston Carey, James Carey 3rd, Millicent Carey McIntosh, Anthony Morris Carey, Jr., and Richard H.T. Carey. He was a Quaker elder and his funeral service was held at the Homewood Friends Meeting House on Charles Street in Baltimore.

Morris was the first President of the Carey Machinery and Supply Company incorporated in 1900 as successor to Thomas K. Carey & Brothers The closely held firm sold and serviced industrial supplies, safety equipment and machine tools to firms in the region such as Bethlehem Steel. His son Richard H.T. Carey, who married Laura Moran, was a store manager for the

Company.

In 1930 upon Morris's death, his eldest son, G. Cheston Carey succeeded as President followed by his son, G. Cheston "Cheddy" Carey Jr. Upon Cheddy Carey's death in 1996, the firm was sold to J. Fegely Inc., of Pottstown, Pennsylvania, an industrial supply firm that promised to retain a majority of the work force and the Carey name.

Because Morris and Margaret were staunch Quaker pacifists, the Company did not accept military contracts during World War II and suffered financially as a result. Of their three sons old enough to serve, two joined the military but never left the country or saw combat. Cheston, the oldest son, was a conscientious objector and served with the American Friends Service Committee as an ambulance driver in France where he found himself as a non-combatant in the midst of military action.

Margaret Carey was an active member of the Homewood Friends and supported a number of social reform and civil rights causes, including obtaining the right of women to vote, the YWCA, race relations, and the peace movement for which she testified before the House of Representatives in 1921 on world disarmament. She chaired the Maryland Civil Liberties Committee, a precursor to the ACLU.

She collaborated with Lillie Carroll Jackson, the head of the Baltimore Branch of the NAACP and members of the Mitchell family, in the struggle for racial equality. She organized interracial meetings at the Baltimore Street YWCA and at her home in the Guildford section of Baltimore City to protest the lynchings on the Eastern Shore of Maryland in the early 1930's and the Jim Crow laws in downtown department stores and public buildings. She served as the Homewood Friends representative

to the Anti-Lynching Federation of Baltimore and in 1937 testified before Congress in support of the Wagner-Costigan anti-lynching legislation. Lillie Carroll Jackson died in 1975 and
under her Will directed that her house on Eutaw Street in Baltimore be made into a civil rights museum and a room dedicated to the memory of Margaret Carey. Morgan State University
now owns and operates the Lillie Carroll Jackson Museum,
which has a room on its second floor dedicated to Margaret
Carey and her family.

Morris and Margaret were the parents of four sons: Galloway Cheston, James Carey3rd, Anthony Morris, Jr., and Richard Henry Thomas and two daughters Margaret Millicent and
Susan Shober who died at an early age.

Galloway Cheston, who used Cheston as his first name, was
born in 1897 and died in 1970. He was President of Carey Machinery & Supply Company for 30 years, a trustee and treasurer
of the Homewood Friends Meeting, member of the board and
Treasurer of Friends House and President of the Miles White
Beneficial Society. He served as the first Chairman of the Housing Authority of Baltimore City at the time in 1954 when the
Authority banned racial discrimination in housing. He was also
a member of the Governor's Commission on Interracial Prob-
lems.

His wife, Margaret Macdonald Fitts was a graduate of the
Baldwin School in Philadelphia and Vassar College. She was
a member of the Board of the Keswick Multi-Care Center for
twenty years and served as its president for three years. The
couple had two children: G. Cheston, Jr., known as "Cheddy"
and Mary Louise.

Cheddy Carey was born in 1930 and died in 1995. He graduated from Princeton University where he was an All American

lacrosse player and member of a national championship team. He was a Fullbright Scholar at the University of Manchester and served in the Navy from 1952 to 1956. A member of the Greater Baltimore Committee, he was on the boards of the Baltimore Symphony Orchestra, Walters Art Gallery, and the City Planning Commission.

Cheddy married Deanne Shutter Beach who died in 1980 and subsequently Clelia Delafield. He had two sons by Deanne Beach: Galloway Cheston Carey III, who lives in Washington, DC, and Geoffrey R.B. Carey, a Principal at the investment firm of Brown Advisory & Trust Company in Baltimore. Geoffrey Carey married Susan Hankin and they are the parents of Charlotte Galbraith Carey and Grant Cheston Carey.

Mary Louise Carey graduated from Bryn Mawr School and Goucher College. She married first W. Conwell Smith and they are the parents of Georgia Donovan Smith, Margaret Carey Smith, Mark Conwell Smith and Deidre Macdonald Smith. Her second husband is Eberhard Faber IV, a Princeton graduate and former President of the Eberhard Faber Pencil Company. The couple live in Bear Creek, Pennsylvania.

James Carey 3rd, the second son of Morris and Margaret Carey was born in 1895 and died in 1964. He attended Gilman School, Haverford College and Harvard Law School. He was a member of the board of Carey Machinery & Supply Company and of the law firm of Brune, Parker, Carey and Gans and later Marshall, Carey and Doub in Baltimore. He was a founder and on the board of the Peale Museum and the Baltimore Museum of Art and helped to establish the 14 West Hamilton Street Club and the Ellicott Graveyard, Inc.

James married first Polly Parker and second Mary Lewis Hall, a portrait painter whose works are exhibited at the National Gallery of Design in New York, the Corcoran Art Gallery, the Phillips Gallery in Washington, D.C. and hang in many buildings in the Baltimore area. In 1956 she assisted Leon Kroll in the execution of six panels of murals in Shriver Hall at Johns Hopkins University.

By Polly, his first wife, James was the father of Reverend James Carey IV who attended Gilman School, Harvard University and General Theological Seminary in New York City. He was ordained as an Episcopal priest and served in churches in Baltimore, Fall River, Massachusetts, and North Providence, Rhode Island.

By his second wife, James Carey was the father of Anne Thomas, a painter and artist who served as Chair of the Maryland Commission on the Status of Women, the Board of Trustees of Morgan State University and as board chair of the Maryland Eye Bank. She married William Boucher III, the Executive Director of the Greater Baltimore Committee. The couple lived for many years at "Bellefield Farm" in the Long Green Valley of Baltimore County, Maryland.

Anthony Morris Carey, Jr., Morris and Margaret Carey's third son was born in 1900 and died in 1964. He attended Calvert and Gilman schools, graduated from Princeton University in 1922 and was a Lieutenant in the Marine Corps during World War II. From 1935 to 1947 he was the head of Carey Sales and Service, a refrigeration firm, and later served as a partner of Carey & Gordon, manufacturers agents.

He married Louise Waterman, a native of Providence, Rhode Island and descendant of Roger Williams. She was a Vice President and head of the horse stables and riding classes for the Humane Society of Baltimore County and a member of the board of the Carroll County Humane Society. She founded and ran Hobby Horse Hall, a kindergarten that featured the humane treatment of animals. Anthony and Louise were the parents of Anthony Morris Carey III and Louise Foster Carey.

Anthony Morris Carey III, born in 1935, graduated from Gilman School, Princeton University and Harvard Law School. He was a partner in the Baltimore Law firm of Venable LLP and later the firm of Shelton & Carey LLP. He served in the U.S. Air Force, as an assistant attorney general for Maryland, Executive Secretary of the Maryland State Board of Ethics and as Special Assistant for Energy with the U.S. Department of Housing and Urban Development. He was a board member of Baltimore Center Stage, the Baltimore Choral Arts Society, and the board of the Bethel Outreach Center. He has been involved with the Baltimore School for the Arts, a public arts high school located in Baltimore City for forty years, as its founding Chairman and President of its supporting Foundation. The School, located in the former Alcazar Hotel building in the Mount Vernon area of Baltimore City was ranked the best public school in Baltimore by the *U.S. News and World Report* and awarded the highest 5-star rating by the Maryland Department of Education, one of only three Baltimore City public schools to receive such a designation.

He married Eleanor Mackey of Providence, Rhode Island in October, 1967. She is a graduate of Classical High School in Providence, Wellesley College and the University of Maryland School of Law. A former associate with the Baltimore law firm of Frank, Bernstein, Conaway and Goldman, she was Deputy Attorney General and ran for Attorney General of Maryland. She served as Special Counselor to the Governor and was subsequently appointed President of the Governor's Workforce Investment Board. She is on the board of the Bethel Outreach

**Rededication of the Lillie Carroll Jackson Museum
and the Margaret T. Carey Room on June 15, 2016**

David Wilson, President of Morgan State University; Eleanor M. (Ellie) Carey, Anthony M. (Tony) Carey, Gabriel Tenabe, Director of the James E. Lewis Museum

Center, a Trustee of the Maryland Historical Society, and currently, as the President of Baltimore Community Rowing, is active in the development of the 11-mile waterfront of the Middle Branch of the Patapsco River. The couple live in downtown Baltimore near the Inner Harbor.

Louise Foster Carey was born in 1936, graduated from the Garrison Forest School in Baltimore County, Goucher College and earned a Master's Degree in Social Work from Bryn Mawr College. She is the former head of the Medical Social Work Department of Cooper Union Hospital in Newark, New Jersey and of Union Memorial Hospital in Baltimore. She married Constantine "Gus" Courpas in 1983, an architect who headed the architectural division of the Maryland Mass Transit Administration.

Margaret Millicent Carey, the surviving daughter of Morris and Margaret Carey, who used Millicent as her first name, was born in 1898 and died in 2001. She was a distinguished educator and advocate for women combining multiple roles. A graduate of Bryn Mawr School in Baltimore, she earned a PhD in English Literature from Johns Hopkins University. She served as the Headmistress of the Brearley, a private girls' school in New York City for 17 years and was appointed Dean of Barnard College, a women's college in New York City affiliated with Columbia University and soon after its first President. In 1932, she married Doctor Rustin McIntosh, a pediatrician who taught at the Columbia College of Physicians and Surgeons and was later director of the New York Babies Hospital. After the couple retired they moved in 1962 to their farm in Tyringham, Massachusetts. They had five children: Rustin Carey, James Henry, Kenneth, Susan Margaret and John Richard, all of whom have had distinguished academic or professional careers.

Much of this family history was presented at the Carey/Cary Family reunion on October 25, 2003.

- Anthony M. (Tony) Carey III

Graduate of Gilman School, Princeton University and Harvard School of Law. He served in the U. S. Air Force, as Assistant Attorney General of Maryland, as Executive Secretary of the Maryland State Board of Ethics and as Special Assistant for Energy with the U.S. Department of Housing and Urban Development. He has been a board member of Baltimore Center Stage, the Baltimore Choral Arts Society, the board of the Bethel Outreach Center, founding Chairman of the Board of Trustees of the Baltimore School for the Arts and President of its supporting foundation.

CHAPTER 12

HOPE AND HISTORY: THE CAREYS AND BEYOND
- *DONALD L. (DON) WARD* -

From Castle Cary in England to Carey's Church and Camp in Delaware, the Carey family has spun a web that is both deep and wide. It is deep because its roots have become intertwined in communities as the Careys have become active, contributing members of society, often in leadership roles. The web is wide because it has covered much of the English-speaking world.

Different branches of the Carey family received grants of land on the Delmarva Peninsula in the 1700s. Some of those grants were in the southern part of Sussex County, Delaware. The reader will find it of interest to explore the interaction between one of those branches in the late 1800s and the Methodist movement that had been growing in the area since the end of the 18th century. The result of this interaction has become an important part of local history, and culture, as well as religious and social life.

> *History says; don't hope on this side of the grave,*
> *but then, once in a lifetime the longed-for tidal*
> *wave of justice can rise up, and hope and history rhyme.*
> *Seamus Haeney*

Some may suggest that the analogy of this poem to the interaction referenced above may contain more than a bit of

154

hyperbole. However, the confluence of two groups of people seeking land to build a house of worship and a landowner willing to donate that land is a prime example of the tidal wave where hope and history rhyme. The result, in this case, affected the lives of thousands over the following century and continues today to have a significant impact on the culture of the area. This may not represent a tidal wave of justice; but the events described here provided the framework for the rhyming of hope and history for those lives that were changed, as well as untold future generations whose lives will be forever impacted because of this story.

Carey's Church, the Beginning

The seeds of hope were sown in the late 1700s when Freeborn Garretson and other Methodist circuit riders were sent by Bishop Francis Asbury across the Delmarva Peninsula in addition to many other areas of the eastern United States to preach the Methodist gospel. Garretson was one of the better known of this group perhaps because he kept an extensive journal. These itinerant preachers carried all their possessions in saddle bags and traveled by horseback down every road and path they could find, preaching to all who would listen. At night, they hoped to find a family sympathetic to their message that would provide food and lodging. Frequently, they preached to individual farmers in the field by day and to groups gathered in homes at night. Thousands of souls were added to the faith, but there were few organized churches in the rural areas. Methodism was, indeed, in its infancy. Its growth depended on the ability of these men to spread the message and increase the number of believers. The churches were first built in the towns since it was easier to assemble a group there. Slowly, the circuit riders moved into the countryside where their preaching was met with considerable resistance since, to the listeners, the message represented radical ideas. The reluctance was, however, quickly overcome; and the faithful were soon measured in the thousands. The success of the men on horseback can be seen today by observing the vast number of Methodist churches in rural Delmarva. This was quite amazing, considering the sparseness of the population in the countryside. In many cases, it was the first time the remote farming community had been exposed to any form of religion. Because south-central Sussex County was one of the more sparsely populated areas of the peninsula, the region was much later in hearing the Methodist gospel.

As a result of the tireless work done by the circuit riders, in the late 1700s small groups called Methodist Societies had begun to form on the peninsula. They met in members' homes, barns, or the one-room schools that dotted the countryside. History is a bit sparse with specifics; however, what it does tell is that for several years, two Methodist Societies were meeting in the area about five miles west of Millsboro. One was the Mission Hill Society meeting in Mission Hill School; and the other was the Phillips Hill Society, meeting in Phillips Hill School. In the mid-1800s these two groups joined together during the late summer holding outdoor gatherings called "bush meetings." They met at a location shown on old maps as Mudford which, ironically, was close to an Indian encampment that existed hundreds of years previously. Staying for several days, the people slept in crude, makeshift tents, as well as in and under wagons. Cooking was done over open fires. The activities included Bible study during the day and religious services during the evening. The meetings, a forerunner of the camp meeting revivals, provided an opportunity to interact with members of other societies and were a significant factor in increasing the religious zeal of this young movement. The worshipers, however, were faced with a conundrum. Everyone hoped to find a way to build a church, but they knew that money was very scarce and funds for such a building would be very difficult to secure. Transportation was slow and cumbersome, so the church needed to be in the proximity of most of the potential congregants. Even though the one-room schools provided a place to meet and worship, they were viewed as temporary and did not fulfill the desire for a permanent place of worship. The people wanted a church! There was plenty of hope, but would history arrive to make a rhyme.

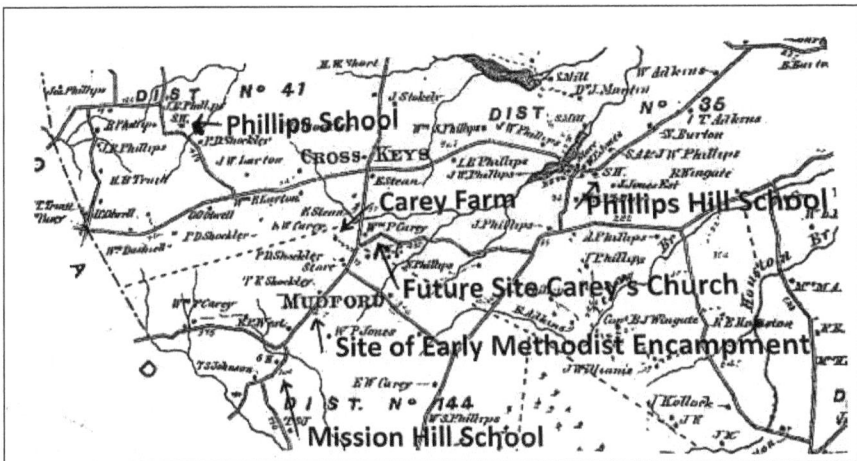

Enlarged Section of 1868 Map of Delaware Showing the Carey Farm, Location of Area Schools, Future Location of Carey's Church and Mudford, Location of First Methodist Encampments

The 1868 map, part of an extensive map of the state of Delaware, shows the location of Mission Hill School and Phillips Hill School (each marked S.H.). The schools provided meeting places for two of the early Methodist Societies started in this area. Also shown is the location of nearby Phillips School, the farm owned by Elijah W. Carey and the future location of Carey's Church, as well as Mudford where the first Methodist encampments were held. There are some other important areas of note on this map. The lane leading to the Elijah W. Carey homestead was on what is now Carey's Camp Road which passes through Mudford. This road was the most important and most traveled road in the area. It was the main road leading from points west and south as far away as Salisbury, Maryland, to points north to Georgetown and east to Millsborough and the Indian River. The fork just west of the present location of Carey's Church determined if traffic would go north or east. The road in front of the future location of Carey's Church is now much straighter than shown on the map. Given the "highways" of that era, all roads led to the future location of Carey's Church. Many present-day roads such as Conaway Road, which is the road in front of Carey's Cemetery, are, of course, not shown because they did not exist at the time.

Elijah W. and Lavinia Carey owned a few hundred acres of land, in the area north of the present-day Carey's Camp Road. Some of the acreage had been in the family from the time of the original land grants. Knowing the desire of the two societies to build a church, the Careys donated "one acre and eight square perches" (totaling slightly over an acre) of land fronting on the same road as Mudford (Carey's Camp Road), about one-half mile to the east. The location was ideal because it was near the most traveled road in the area and close to most of the potential congregants. History had met hope; and in the hearts and minds of the people, they rhymed quite well.

In 1884, the land was deeded to the Trustees of the Shortly Circuit of the Methodist Episcopal Church, a group of churches nearby that shared a minister. This new Methodist congregation now had land for a church. The future seemed promising; however, the path forward, while filled with hope, was not to be smooth. A building contractor was hired; the foundation and cornerstone (1886) were laid; and construction was begun. Unfortunately, the plans for the new church had not included the necessary fundraising; and money was very, very scarce. The majority of the potential members were poor farm families. Oral history reveals that because the contractor could not be paid, a lien was placed on the church property. Construction came to a halt. In order to prevent foreclosure, the trustees had the church incorporated in Sussex County, February 5, 1891. Interestingly, the church was incorporated as Carey's Methodist Episcopal Church. This is the first time the Carey name appears in any of the historical records related to the church. One of the trustees at the time of this incorporation was Ulysses G. Carey, the grandson of Elijah W. and Lavinia Carey. Slowly funds were raised to complete the structure; and in July, 1891, the first Methodist pastor was appointed to Carey's Methodist Episcopal Church. The new church was soon assigned to the Gumboro Charge which included Westwoods, Gumboro, and Bethel. In 1930, Carey's was combined with Grace Methodist to constitute the Millsboro charge. In 1995, Carey's United Methodist Church became a single-station church no longer sharing a minister. Unfortunately, Elijah W. Carey died in 1887 and was never able to witness the rhyming of hope and history of which he was such an important part.

The first church building was much smaller than the structure today, measuring only about 28 feet wide by 36 feet deep. In front of the church were hitching posts for the horses. Most of the early congregants lived nearby and could walk to church, which many people did, or they could come by horse and buggy. The double wooden doors entering the current sanctuary and the glass panel above them are believed to be original. There were two woodstoves in the first church, one on each side of the sanctuary. Four aisles, one along each outside wall and one on either side of a row of long benches in the center, provided access to the front of the church. The benches near the outside walls were much shorter, and two were left out on each side for the wood stoves. There was a large wooden box in back of each wood stove containing firewood which could be added to the stove as needed during the service. Someone in the congregation volunteered to go to the church early on Sunday morning in the winter and start the fire in the wood stoves. There was no electricity; so in the summer the windows were raised for cooling. No one had plumbing at home; thus there was no thought of having it at church. Prior to the addition of the church house in 1957, there were outside primitive toilets available that were also used for camp meeting in the summer. The windows of the church had wooden shutters outside which were opened and closed for each service.

Sunday School records reveal that growth over the first forty years was quite remarkable. The record book for Sunday, June 27, 1926, for example, shows an attendance of 145 scholars, 9 teachers, and 18 visitors, with the total present of 172 and the total collection of $5.01. Yes, that was the collection for the entire congregation! Such attendance was most incredible considering the available church space was less than 1,100 square feet. Where did everyone sit? Surely, more space was desperately needed.

In 1933, the far wall of the church (behind the pulpit) was moved twelve feet back; a choir loft was constructed; and a large adjacent Sunday School room was added adjoining the sanctuary with very tall folding doors supported by a large steel truss. This addition increased the available space by more than 100 percent and provided ample room for a large youth department with several Sunday School classes. Four adult classes were conducted in the sanctuary, each having a different teacher. One of the interesting practices at some churches, including Carey's, was giving tickets weekly to each youth who attended Sunday School. While most churches did not give tickets, at Carey's it was believed this would be an incentive for the youth to attend Sunday School. The tickets could be redeemed each year at the annual Sunday School picnic for one cent each. If that does not seem like much, remember that a penny could actually buy something then and with five of them you could even get a candy bar.

Carey's Camp

What happened to the bush meetings that were taking place in late summer at Mudford? All that is known for certain is that those meetings, which came to be called camp meetings, were moved about a half mile away to a site in "a grove of Oaks" adjacent to Carey's Church. Exactly when this happened is unclear, but it seems to have taken place shortly after the church was completed. In 1908, a parcel adjacent to the church was purchased by the trustees for $498.44 from Elijah W. Carey's grandson, Ulysses G. Carey, who had been a member of Carey's since 1892. Whatever the time line, church families built 47 crude one-and-a-half story, cabin-like structures with a modest kitchen in the back. These buildings had an open living area extending into a porch in the front so that each one faced the tabernacle which was in the center of the camp ground. Sleeping quarters were upstairs. Each family tried to give their cabin a bit of identity. One way they accomplished this was to string crepe paper across the porch, sometimes adding multiple colors and fancy designs. During the encampment, friends and family would gather in the main room or on the porch each evening to listen to the singers and preachers, or they could join the congregation in the tabernacle.

This structure was originally rectangular but was modified later to the shape of a cross. The original seats were blocks of wood or boards resting on logs, none of which had a back. How uncomfortable, especially for a long sermon! Later benches were added and finally seats when some local schools and later one of the Sussex County offices were remodeled. The original tabernacle, showing signs of age, was replaced by a modern structure in 2000; but the character of the old building was maintained. The new worship area was designed by Wayne Tull using trusses which, unlike the original, provided a clear span with no obstructions. When the meetings were at Mudford, the living accommodations were crude tents made of canvas or sheets stretched over poles or tree branches. At the new location, the structures which resembled rustic cabins were called "tents" since that was the familiar name at Mudford. The reference to the living quarters at the new location as tents seemed to stick like iron on a magnet. For the next century and beyond, the name never changed!

Today, when someone refers to the "cabins," the locals smile and welcome those who are clearly visitors. Interestingly, every year at camp the question arises from some visitors, "How do I get one of these cabins?" The locals politely reply, "You don't." The tents are considered family treasures and are usually passed down from one generation to the next. During the last decade several owners have replaced their "tents" with new ones.

The camp meeting in many ways still is the focal point of social life in the community during the encampment time of late July and early August. This time was originally chosen to accommodate farm life. Farmers had planted and cultivated their crops but harvest was weeks away.

There has been much speculation about the demise of camp meetings. In the beginning, modes of transportation restricted traveling distances for any type of event. Since there were very few events taking place, the only large gatherings were the camp meetings. They became essentially the only "show in town." The change in transportation marked the beginning of the decline of these popular gatherings. In addition, many of the early meetings were plagued with alcohol-related, disruptive behavior which some camps found difficult to address. Bare knuckle fistfights were a common pastime of that era for young men. What better place to test skills and claim bragging rights in this sport than at a camp meeting where a large crowd was guaranteed. Every night there were dozens of such fights at most camps. Some of the camp meetings were closed because they were unable to cope with these disruptions. Other camp closures seem to have been related to a lack of leadership or a strong connection with a church. With all the ambiguity about the closure of camp meetings, one point that seems clear is that Carey's continues to thrive and seems well positioned to move forward into the future as one of the few camp meetings in Delaware to survive. Several years ago, a Delaware Historical Marker was erected at Carey's Camp indicating that it was a site of historic interest.

In the early years, the congregation of Carey's Church,

hoped that they would grow and become a beacon for the message of Christ and the Methodist faith. For over a century, the Thomas Jones family, more than any other group, has provided the history that made that hope become real. This story, however, has yet another twist.

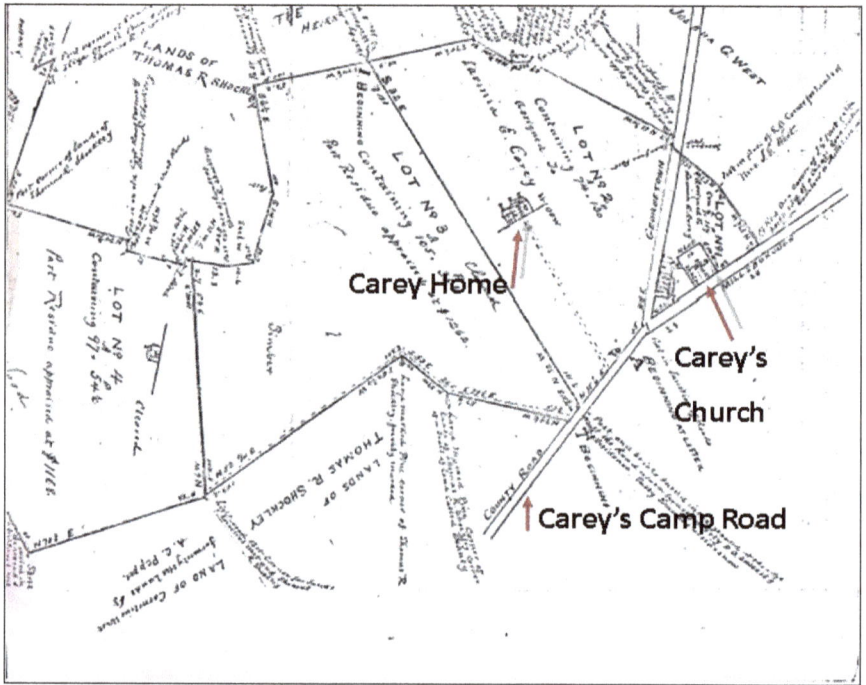

Carey Home

Carey's Church

Carey's Camp Road

Carey Farm Survery

What Became of the Carey Homestead?

As can be seen from the above survey, the lands owned by the Elijah W. Carey family were divided into four parcels (shown as lots on the survey). The homestead with a two-story, post-and-beam constructed home (circa late 1700s) was located on Lot Two.

In the decades following Elijah W. Carey's death, the Carey land holdings were sold in separate parcels. A few acres were sold to Carey's Church in 1909. In 1925, the homestead containing approximately 74 acres, located across what is now Cross Keys Road from the church, was purchased by a local farmer, Jesse Brittingham, for his daughter and son-in-law, Myrtle and Elmer Wootten. When Elmer Wootten died a few years later, Jesse was interested in selling the farm. Elmer Ward, a member of Carey's Church and a grandson of Thomas Jones, had recently married Florence Rogers; and they were hoping to find a farm near his parents since Elmer was share-cropping with his father, George. The newly married couple had an age-old problem; they had a lot of hope but no money. Would hope and history rhyme again?

When Elmer expressed an interest in buying the farm from Jesse Brittingham, he shared the couple's financial situation--they had no money! Jesse made the young couple what seems today an incredible offer. He agreed to sell them the homestead for $1,500 at three percent interest, which was due annually. The principal could be paid at the discretion of the purchasers; in other words, whatever and whenever they could pay. The Wards accepted the offer and with great anticipation moved into what was the Carey two-story house on Lot Two. Ironically, with no money down, the grandson of Thomas Jones bought 74 acres and the home of Thomas' friend, Elijah W. Carey. Hope and history met again! Surely the rhyme continued. As a special note, the only structure still existing from Elijah W. Carey's homestead is the hand-hewn, cedar corn crib that was donated to the Delaware Agriculture Museum in Dover, Delaware, by Florence Ward in 1974 after her husband Elmer died.

The Story Continues

This story, like all history, will never end. Almost sixty years after Elmer and Florence Ward bought what was the Carey homestead, their son, Donald, was serving as lay leader of Carey's Church. The Carey family, including the descendants of Elijah W. Carey, was planning their first reunion in 1994. Niel Carey, heading up the reunion, contacted Ralph Dorey, a longtime trustee of Carey's Church, about the group's attending a service at the church. What better way to end a weekend reunion than to worship together at the little country church whose name they shared. Lay leader, Donald Ward (Don as he was known) was involved in coordinating the Carey family visit and introducing them to the congregation. While doing so, he shared a bit of history, and explained to the congregation why the visitors had decided to worship at Carey's. The congregation welcomed the visitors and graciously provided a luncheon for all after the worship service.

The annual reunion worship services and luncheons have, over the past 25 years, become much more than a church service followed by a meal. Friendships have been made. Those friendships have become relationships which have become bonding experiences. Another sometimes overlooked spinoff of this relationship has been the advancement of knowledge and the preservation of history. The Carey reunions have frequently been held at the Nabb Center located in the new library at Salisbury University in Salisbury, Maryland. The Nabb Center has become a phenomenal repository of Delmarva history, folklore, and genealogical information. As a part of the Carey family weekend reunion, participants have had an opportunity to explore the facility and have been joined by individuals knowledgeable about various aspects of local history.

Don, the author, who is not a direct family member, has been a guest at several of the reunions and has been impressed with the information presented.

During one of those reunion sessions, the attendees learned that the Nabb Center was in the process of forming a collection of oral histories recorded from individuals on the Delmarva Peninsula who possessed unique knowledge from the past and were willing to share. When Don learned about the program and realized no one was recording these histories with a focus on Sussex County, Delaware, he immediately volunteered to become a recorder for this project. Several audio recordings focusing on Sussex County are now in the Naab center as a direct result of information provided at the annual reunion of the Carey family. An example of the urgency in making the recordings is sadly demonstrated by the deaths of three individuals who passed shortly after completing an audio recording of their early memories in Sussex County. This project is a valuable effort toward preserving early memories of Carey's Church and Camp and life in rural Sussex County several decades ago. Sadly, the Grim Reaper frequently arrives before the recorder as has happened so many times in the past.

This chapter has been a snippet of history for a tiny part of Sussex County looking back more than two centuries. It is, however, in a much greater sense, so much more. The product of hope, unselfish action, and endless opportunities produce an unending litany of change reaching far beyond anyone's imagination. It is only when hope and action are forged in the fire of persistence that seemingly impossible dreams come true. Actions, good or evil, are never an end unto themselves.

There are always unforeseen consequences or benefits; and as this chapter has demonstrated, sometimes they never seem to end. Perhaps no one said it better than the poet, James Foley, when he penned these lines:

Drop a Pebble in the Water

Drop a pebble in the water: just a splash, and it is gone;
But there's half-a-hundred ripples circling on and on and on,
Spreading, spreading from the center, flowing on out to the sea.
And there is no way of telling where the end is going to be.

Drop a pebble in the water: in a minute you forget,
But there's little waves a-flowing, and there's ripples circling yet,
And those little waves a-flowing to a great big wave have grown;
You've disturbed a mighty river just by dropping in a stone.

Epilogue

Is there a moral to this story, or is it just a bit of historical trivia? Is there a veiled message embedded for which the reader must search? Does history really tell us, "Don't hope on this side of the grave?" Hope is the seed of history. What event in history did not begin with hope--hope for a better life, hope for freedom? Sometimes those with power hope for more. If a seed is to develop, it must be watered and, as the scripture tells, "fall on good soil." Perhaps the message of history is that hope alone, without water, good soil, and nurture will sometimes drift into oblivion. But the great and small ideas of history begin with hope. That seed that lives within all of us sometimes remains dormant, but sometimes it violently explodes with the belief that hope can become reality.

Other early Methodist societies in the area wanted to have

a church, but they were unsuccessful. What made the difference? Was it the absence of a land owner to step up and make hope and history rhyme? There were other farm families who hoped to own a farm but never did, perhaps because there was no one to offer them credit as one farmer did.

Is there something in this story beyond history? Of course there is. If germinal ideas of hope are to succeed, another force is needed, a facilitating force that can provide the history to complete the rhyme. What can be the origin of such a force? Anyone can!

- Donald L. (Don) Ward

Donald L.(Don) Ward, a retired educator, lives on the original Lot Two of the Elijah W. Carey farm. He spent his first twelve years growing up in the original Carey two-story, post-and-beam home. He descended from four generations of local sharecroppers on his grandfather Ward's side of the family. As a youngster he occasionally accompanied his grandfather to Carey's Church early on Sunday mornings in the winter and "helped" start the fires in the wood stoves. Joining Carey's Church at the age of twelve, he has been a lifelong member. He is hopeful for the future of Carey's Church and is blessed to be a part of "The Little Church with A Big Heart."

SECTION 3

SUPPORTING AND STRENGTHENING THE CAREY/CARY FAMILY ORGANIZATION

CHAPTER 13

FAMILY HISTORY CENTERS

RICHARD G. (RICK) AND BARBARA P. CAREY

Genealogy, the study of one's ancestors or family history, is one of the most popular hobbies in the world. Since 1894, The Church of Jesus Christ of Latter-day Saints has dedicated time and resources to collecting and sharing records of genealogical importance. Due to cooperation from government archives, churches, and libraries, the Church has created the largest collection of family records in the world, with information on more than 3 billion deceased people. This effort was originally facilitated through FamilySearch, a non-profit organization sponsored by the Church. FamilySearch provides access to information from 100 countries, including birth, marriage, and death records, censuses, probates and wills, land records, and more. These records are made available to the public free of charge through the FamilySearch.org website, the world-renowned Family History Library in Salt Lake City, and through a network of local family history centers in 126 countries.

Recently I was called by the leadership of the Church along with my wife Barbara to be co-Directors of the Family History Center in our unit of the Church in Wilmington, Delaware. We both had been volunteers at the Center over the years. When I started my family research in 1984, the family History Center is where I started. At that time before the popularity of computers most research was done with microfilm and microfiche. There were not as many FHC's available as there are today. Now most of the microfilm has been or is in the process of being indexed and made available on the internet. Each FHC has different materials available. Before I review the records to which the public may access, , let me share what is on FamilySearch.

When you login to FamilySearch you will notice The Family History Center Services portal where you will find Premium Family History Websites, no charge to Patrons. These websites can only be accessed at a FHC. Sites available include Newspaper Archives, War Records starting with the The Revolutionary War, some published Family Histories and Genealogies, My Heritage with more being added in the future. Other sites available include The Family History Guide--a free, comprehensive learning and resource center about family history and FamilySearch.

- My Family Booklet: Capture and preserve your family story.
- FamilySearch Blog: FamilySearch news and helpful tips.
- FamilySearch Wiki: Free family history research advice for the community, by the community.
- FamilySearch Help Center: FamilySearch knowledge center.

Anyone can volunteer to help with indexing at any FHC or from the comfort of your home. A link is found on the FamilySearch home page.

Equipment available at the Centers also varies by location. At our Center in Wilmington we have 5 Microfilm readers, 1 Microfiche reader, 1 Microfilm/Microfiche scanner for copies, 6 computers and a copier/printer.

Other items you would find at our Center would be a large collection of microfilms covering records from The Catholic Diocese of Wilmington, Delaware, some as far back as the mid 1700's. These include:

- Baptism, Church membership, Death and Cemetery records.
- Microfiche: Old parochial Registers of Scotland.
- 1881 Census Indexes: England, Wales, Channel Islands and Isle of Mann.

We also have several hundred assorted indefinite microfilms covering many Places and Topics AND Misc Geneological research books-- some family histories that patrons have donated over the years.

This is just a sampling of what you might find at other Family History Centers. There are always volunteers to help and guide you in your research.

- Richard G. and Barbara P. Carey

Editor's Note: Carey/Cary Family members and researchers have accessed and found the Family History Center resources very useful and the Center staff very helpful. At the same time, we have shared Carey/Cary Family information and research with the Church of Jesus Christ of Latter Day Saints. Specifically, Rick and Barbara personally carried a copy of the bound Carey/Cary Newsletters to the Family History Library in Salt Lake City.

CHAPTER 14

CAREY / CARY FAMILY: WEBSITE AND DNA PROJECT
- E. NIEL CAREY, HELEN S. CAREY AND SEAN GILSON -

The Carey/Cary Family website www.careycary.org has been an important tool for communicating with Carey/Cary Family members and friends, for sharing family research, and for providing information about our family organization and an opportunity for interested persons to become members. Our Carey/Cary DNA Project has enabled male family members to engage in the DNA testing process and to use the test results to identify their family lineage, to identify family relationships and also share that information with other Carey/Cary Family members and friends.

Fortunately, after he joined the organization Sean Gilson agreed to establish and maintain the Carey/Cary Family website and later, as he participated in the DNA testing process, also agreed to inform family members of the advantages of DNA testing and encouraged them to participate in its Carey/Cary DNA Project. Sean's interest in Carey/Cary Family genealogy, his active membership in several genealogical organization, and his professional expertise in information systems technology have enabled him to organize and manage the website and the DNA project, while at the same time, managing increasing his personal family and work responsibilities. The website features extensive information about the Carey/Cary Family organization, its history and goals, information about the annual family reunion, and a section containing a complete collection of the archived Carey/Cary Family newsletters. In terms of the newsletter collection, , it was decided that, after the website was established, the latter would be the primary communications tool for the organization. While the newsletter would no longer be published, a complete set of existing newsletters would be available on the website for future use and reference.

The website has proved to be an effective means of sharing information about our family organization and for providing a means by which interested persons could become members. During the time our organization has been in existence we have had family members from nineteen states while members from sixteen of these states have attended one or more Carey/Cary Family reunions. We have received queries about particular ancestral individuals which Helen seeks to answer directly or after consultation wih other resources. This process often leads to a new member of the organization, who then sometimes shares important information and/or attends our reunion. In addition, after we ceased to publish newsletters we fortunately were able to archive the fourteen years of timeless newsletters on the web site. We also have been able to place information about a CareyCary research project about Peter Carey, and establish a link with Ancestry for sharing information. The project has had positive results.

After Sean Gilson completed the DNA test he gained valuable information about his own Carey/Cary Family roots. As he shared his information, the Carey/Cary Family Board asked him to organize and manage the Carey/Cary DNA project which he agreed to do. The Carey/Cary DNA project is affiliated with the much larger Carey/Cary DNA project which is managed by Dr. John Carey.

As of September 1, 2019, we have the following DNA test information for the Carey Cary DNA Project.

At this time we have 245 members in the Carey/Cary DNA Surname Project. We continuously post new results for members and we are in the process of checking for new matches in the project. We have project members from Haplogroups E, G, I, R1a and R1b. Most members are from Haplogroup R1b.

Many project members do not have DNA matches within the project so we are unable to assign them to lineages. However, we have been able to identify twelve lineages from matches within the project, as follows:

Haplogroup I - Lineage I. We have one project member for this lineage. Michael Kary from DurmersheimBaden-Wuerttemberg Germany is the suspected ancestor for this lineage.

Haplogroup I - Lineage II. We have three project members for this lineage. Peter Carey b. 1698 from Paulerspury Northhamptonshire England is the suspected ancestor for this lineage.

Haplogroup R1a - Lineage I. We have three project members who are in this lineage. One member has identified an earliest ancestor as James H Carey b. 1813 in Delaware and provided a pedigree which is on our About/news page. The second identifies the ancestor as David or John Carey from Worcester County, MD, born circa 1800. The third has identified an earliest ancestor who does not have the Carey but a Parsons surname.

Haplogroup R1b - Lineage I. We have eleven project members in this lineage and three more possible members. One has provided a pedigree with an earliest ancestor John Cary born in Bristol, England, circa 1610 who immigrated to Massachusetts in the earlY-1600s. The other has an earliest known ancestor born in New York circa 1808. Comparative analysis of the haplotype for these two members suggests that their earliest most recent common ancestor lived before John Cary emigrated from England.

Haplogroup Rlb - Lineage II. We have ten project members who are from this lineage and one possible member with 12 markers which gives us the beginnings of a pretty good model for this lineage. Most have identified that their earliest ancestor was Thomas Cary who emigrated from England or Scotland to the United States in the 1660s, living first in Virginia and then Maryland. Based on the pedigree information they provided we have a posted a combined pedigree that links most of them on our About/news page. Comparative analysis of the haplotypes for these members supports the pedigree.

Haplogroup Rlb - Lineage III. We have eight project members in this lineage and one possible member with 12 markers. Seven of the members indicate either James or John Carey of Virginia as the ancestor of these lineages. The eighth member has a pedigree that connects to the Carey family of the Guernsey Channel Islands where there have been Careys since the 1300s.

Haplogroup Rlb - Lineage IV. We have two project members in this lineage. Earliest ancestor is from County Tipperary and county Mayo Ireland.

Haplogroup Rlb - Lineage V. We have six project members in this lineage. It is suspected that their earliest ancestor was Jonathon Cary born circa 1711 in Maryland which had at least two sons named Solomon and Peter. There is also a possibility of a son named Jonathan.

Haplogroup R1b =Lineage VI. NOT BEING USED CURRENTLY

Haplogroup R1b - Lineage VII. We have two project members in this lineage. The ancestor to this line is John Carey b. 1680 Buckinghamshire England who migrated to Bucks County, PA.

Haplogroup R1b - Lineage VIII. We have three project members in this lineage. All of them have identified a connection to the Bahamas. Both have indicated that their earliest known ancestor was a William Carey born in the Bahamas circa 1840.

Haplogroup R1b - Lineage IX. We have two project members for this lineage. James Carey from Newport ParishTipperary/Limerick Ireland and Thomas Carew/Carey from KilcommonTipperary Ireland are the suspected ancestors for this lineage.

Haplogroup R1b - Lineage X. We have three project members for this lineage. William Carey b. circa 1790 Ireland, Anthony Carey b. circa 1811 Castlebar Mayo Ireland , and Anthony Carrey b. ?1755 Scotland or Carrickfergus Antrim Ireland are the suspected ancestors for this lineage.

If you are interested in DNA testing, contact Sean Gilson (scgilson@gmail.com). If you have DNA test results or a pedigree, please share them with Sean. Sean recently compiled the following DNA test information and has shared it with Carey/Cary Family members.

In summary, the Carey/Cary Family website has undoubtedly drawn attention to our organization, increased our membership, and encouraged interaction with family members. The Carey/Cary DNA Project has provided valuable information to those family members who are doing family research and has often established or verified family relationships.

CHAPTER 15

THE NABB CENTER AND FAMILY RESEARCH
- *CRESTON LONG, PhD* -

The Edward H. Nabb Research Center for Delmarva History and Culture has been devoted to the study of the region since its founding in 1982. In the Nabb Center's facility in the Guerierri Academic Commons, students, community researchers, and visiting scholars have the opportunity to advance their study of the region for the next generation. The Carey Family Research Room houses the Center's general book collection and its microfilm holdings and has seating for 50 researchers. On any given day, someone visiting the Research Room might find students working on class research assignments, scholars searching archival collections for evidence connected to their research pursuits, or family researchers from as far away as Texas, Arizona, and California, making connections in their family histories. At its core, the Nabb Center is a place where people come to study the past.

One of the most important roles of the Nabb Center involves interpreting the area's history and culture for the campus and the greater community. Its exhibit space allows the Center to carry out this portion of its mission in new and innovative ways. In the entrance to the Nabb Center, the Nieman Gallery houses the permanent Nabb Center exhibit, "Delmarva: People, Place and Time." This exhibit gives a brief history of the region focusing on how Delmarva residents have lived and worked on the land and water from the seventeenth through the twentieth centuries. Telling the story of our region with photographs, documents, and artifacts often requires hours of research for each item in the exhibit. The Nabb Center's Exhibits and Artifacts Curator, arranges the photographs, artifacts and other materials to create an interesting narrative about the central theme of the exhibit. In addition to the permanent exhibit space, the Nabb Center also creates and maintains exhibits in the Thompson Gallery on the fourth floor of the GAC and the space near the first floor east entrance to the GAC. Exhibits in these spaces focus on specific themes and rotate every semester. As the Nabb Center moves forward, the exhibits will be a central feature of our efforts to connect the strength of our research collections with public presentations of our past.

From the start of the Nabb Center, the local history collections have been at the heart of its mission to promote the study of the region's past. As the Center moved into new space in the 1990s, its collections continued to grow and diversify. In addition to the thousands of microfilmed public records, including land, probate and judicial records that date to the 1600s, the Local History Archives makes the Nabb Center a unique regional history repository. Featuring collections from Delaware, Maryland, and Virginia, the Local History Archives truly stands out as the premier manuscript collection featuring materials from all of Delmarva's constituent states. The Local History Archivist maintains the collection and supervises the processing of new collections. As community members, and occasionally other community organizations, donate collections to the Center, the archivist begins processing the collection to make it accessible for researchers. Processing a collection involves a painstaking sequence of steps to arrange or re-arrange materials to put them in an order that is most consistent with their natural or original creation. The ultimate goal is to enable researchers to get the most out of the collections. Students interested in work in public history find great opportunities to work in the Nabb Center archives through internships and student assistant positions. Every semester assistants and interns gain valuable work experience from this training especially if they decide to pursue careers in archival or other information management work, and they also wind up as better, more mindful researchers.

The Nabb Center is also home to the University Archives and Special Collections. The University Archives includes documents, photographs, films, and artifacts connected to Salisbury University's past. With items dating to the founding of the school in the 1920s as Maryland State Normal School, the University Archives is a resource for the campus offices, students, alumni groups and the surrounding community. The University Archivist and Special Collections Librarian supervises this section of the Nabb Center's holdings and works to establish connections with faculty members to promote student use of the Special Collections. Recently, the university archivist supervised the inventorying, rehousing, and assessing the quality of the 649 copies of the *Evergreen* yearbook that are spread throughout the University Archives collections, the Nabb Center stacks and the general library stacks in preparation for their digitization. The University Archives also has uploaded all 329 historical editions in files with their associated metadata into SU's institutional repository. These images of SU's first student newspaper richly illuminate student life at the university from its earliest days and they reveal the interesting story of changes through 1970. They are now freely available online.

With the unique combination of public records such as land and judicial records and the diverse, and ever growing, manuscripts archives, students, community researchers, and visiting scholars can pursue answers to an almost limitless set of questions about the region's history and culture. For instance, the Center has recently been compiling data about the appearance of area Native Americans in the colonial county courts. In the early volumes of the Somerset County court proceedings, it was common for Indians, usually unnamed, to appear in court accused of minor crimes. As the century neared its end, however, Indians more often went to court as plaintiffs asking for relief from white settler encroachment on Indian lands. During this same period, area Indian tribes were being confined more and more to reservation lands, the closest of which was the Tundotank reservation, a mile south of SU's campus today, on Tony Tank Lake. This information reveals a part of the area's history that is mostly left out of popular memory. Our hope is that this sort of research will in time bring some forgotten events back to life. In another example of the Center's efforts to promote research on the region, Aaron Horner, the Center's full-time research assistant, is supervising an ongoing project aimed at understanding the evolution of Delmarva's transportation network. From the earliest days of colonial settlement when the Chesapeake Bay and its tributary rivers and creeks served as the main thoroughfares of the area through the mid-nineteenth-century when efforts to extend railroad lines across the Peninsula came to completion, the story of how people in the region have traveled and transported goods is vital for understanding the area's history.

Dedication of the Academic Commons Facility, September 2016
Including the Nabb Research Center & the Carey Family Research Room

L-R Front: Dr. Creston Long, Director, Nabb Center; Dean of Libraries
and Instructional Resources, Dr. Bea Hardy; Joyce Burrell, Austin Okie;
Niel and Helen Carey.

For years, the Nabb Center has attracted family researchers from across the country as they trace their roots to the
earliest years of English settlement on Delmarva. The vast
collection of microfilmed public records as well as hundreds of
indexes, published family histories and other family lineage-fo-
cused research files have enabled genealogists to make important research connections that have eluded them at other archives. The Leslie Dryden collection has also proven to be an
indispensable resource for countless family researchers. Compiled by Mr. Leslie Dryden, a genealogist of inexhaustible pa-
tience and attention to detail, in the 1960s and 70s, the Dryden
Collection represents a singular effort to index references to
family names in the public records of Lower Delmarva. While

it takes some time to become acclimated to Mr. Dryden's hand-writing, countless researchers have consulted his work to help them overcome obstacles in their family research.

As the Nabb Center moves forward it remains steadfast to its mission of promoting the study of Delmarva's history.

- Creston Long

Editor's note: The Carey/Cary Family reunion has been held at the Nabb Center for th past several years, enabling family members to become familiar with the Nabb Center's extensive collections and to benefit from the Centers very competent and helpful staff.

CHAPTER 16

ALONG THE WAY, CAREY/CARY FAMILY NEWSLETTER
AND A THIRD BLOOD LINE
- HELEN SIMMONS CAREY -

ALONG THE WAY, CAREY/CARY FAMILY NEWSLETTER
AND A THIRD BLOOD LINE
- HELEN SIMMONS CAREY -

Part 1: Along the Way...

Comments were included in my earlier chapter about what preceded the development of my interest in research of Carey/Cary family history. Now it seems appropriate to expand that look…

First, in 1923 my father moved nearby to the small town of Opp to establish a law office where none existed, soon joined by his bride. As his law partner my grandfather (and grandmother) eventually moved to Opp. My father continued in the legal field throughout his life, or almost, for he lived until he was in his hundredth year. As far as 'life lessons' my parents stressed high standards and emphasized quality in outcome, whatever the task. My father thought it important for me to take typing as a high school elective so I would not have to use his "hunt and peck" on the keyboard, for which I have been thankful. I benefited from routine exposure to legal terms, including knowledge about what is meant by terms such as "first cousin, once removed" as well as many others. Such exposure has proved to be valuable in my research experiences.

Further, in the early 1990's a distant "researcher" cousin from out of state and I established contact. Also, it was about that time that computers replaced typewriters to a great extent, and e-mails with attachments began to replace mailed documents, etc. The change in technology made a dramatic and positive difference, in my opinion.

Another factor in my 'research development' is the availability of on-line records, which has replaced many previously necessary trips to libraries or archives. At an earlier time I had regarded it as an advantage to be able to access the National Archives in DC, DAR Library in DE, MD Hall of Records in Annapolis, Maryland, or Nabb Center for Delmarva History and Culture in Salisbury, Maryland--by car, bus, and/or metro.

In retrospect it seems that about this time in my 'development' it was 'off and running' in respect to family history research with one exception—that of having enough time for all in which I had an interest. My responsibility as editor for the Carey/Cary newsletter was an additional factor, although it turned out to be a learning and productive experience beyond my expectations... Never in my "wildest dreams" did I have the expectation that the final outcome of the "newsletter project" would have had such a positive result!

Part 2: Carey/Cary Family Newsletter and Its Beginning

When the Carey/Cary Family Organization was established more than twenty-five years ago the group not only agreed to plan an annual reunion, but "recommended the publication of a newsletter", as reported in its first issue in January 1995. This purpose was not only adopted as a means of communication, etc., but also was to serve as "a historical record of information and about the Carey/Cary family" and to "provide genealogical information which will help family members gather and preserve family lore."

Although initially Rick and Barbara Carey, Rodger Cary,

and Helen Carey accepted the responsibility for the newsletter, within a short time organizational responsibilities were more or less shifted among the group and Rodger discontinued his involvement. Consequently I assumed newsletter responsibility, which evolved into service as its editor, publisher, printer—more or less, all things to all issues... I was able to create the newsletter on Microsoft Word by using extensive formatting. Eventually I learned how to insert pictures, which added interest to the issues. Over the years as Word's versions changed, re-learning its techniques was necessary.

When each issue was complete we had the 8 ½ x 11 sheets copied professionally, as a bi-fold on 11x17 sheets. I prepared mailing labels from the organization's membership database which I developed as an outgrowth of treasurer responsibility. By using team effort Niel helped out with folding, labeling, stamping, and sealing when issues were completed. He always provided encouragement and support in the entire process.

The newsletters now archived on www.careycary.org reflect the newsletter development from the original four-page issue to as many as twelve pages. In addition to those written by the editor, articles were written by other CareyCary members, i.e., Niel Carey, Rick Carey, the late David Carey, Carol Kinney Grimes, Sean Carey Gilson, the late Alvin Carey, Lee Carey Dobson, the late Margaret C. Sherkey, Rear Admiral James J, Carey, Gerry Kaye, Shayne Henderson, and Tom Beggs, in addition to Rebecca Miller and Steve Zender.

We were also fortunate to have several articles voluntarily written by professional researcher Clifford Marion Carey, Ph.D., of Brainerd, MN, who died in 2000. In addition, Norman G. Patterson of Richfield, MN (known for his genealogical research and writing) regularly shared information with the editor. Unfortunately he died in 2001 in a family cemetery in Nodaway County, MO; although at an advanced age, he was singly on a trip to research his family history.

With regularity newsletters included four columns: (1) *Carey/Cary Family: Births, Deaths, and Marriages*, (2) *Query Page: Carey/Cary;* (3) *From the Editor;* and (4) our CareyCary President's *Dear Family and Friends*. Information for obituaries was submitted by members while as editor I regularly scanned newspapers for Carey/Cary items. It was not unusual for my personal friends to send obituaries from their location. Query information was also forwarded by members, although I edited them for publication, based on space available.

In addition to newsletter purposes as outlined in the first paragraph of this Part II, an interest of Carey/Cary researchers and the Editor regularly relate to documentation of Thomas Cary's heritage. The geographical focal point of the newsletter in Delmarva is in sync with Thomas Carey's location when he first appeared in MD records in 1666. We know that a substantial number of first and second generation descendants, by his second wife, were initially living in Delmarva, which in turn points to the likelihood that at least some current day descendants still exist in the same general area and somewhat beyond.

However, as a result of DNA a second Carey/Cary line with a focal point in present-day Wicomico/Somerset/Worcester area has been identified, although some of the line was previously identified as having been in the Whaleyville/Bishopville area in the 1700-1800's.

Finally, the Carey/Cary newsletter publication led to communication with other researchers and has continued, even after its publication ended. Fortunately all fourteen years of issues are now archived on our web site, www.careycary.org , thanks to Sean Gilson. In addition, thanks to "an assist" at the Nabb Center at Salisbury University all issues were bound in a volume, followed by our distribution to a number of libraries in the United States with genealogical emphasis.

Part 3: A Third Blood Line in Milton, DE...

As a preface we should revert to the reference in my earlier chapter that a seemingly third Carey line existed in the Milton, DE, area.

The initial blood line was that of Thomas Cary, the Immigrant, who first appeared in Maryland records in 1666. Three of his children and descendants have been reported in Alfred B. Carey's monograph (referenced in my previous chapter) as having lived in Sussex County, Delaware (including Milton). The children were John, Edward, and Joseph.

Previous reference has been made to Governor Joseph Maull Carey of Wyoming, who was born in Milton, DE. He was descended from John Carey (b. 1665), son of Thomas Cary, and wife Bridget.

According to information provided by descendants the second Carey blood line in Sussex County, DE, was that of James H Carey (1813-1887) and wife Mary Atkins.

Their children included Catherine Eleanor (b, 1831, married Robinson; Henry W. Carey; James Tull Carey (1838-1928); and Joseph Fillmore Carey (b. 1856).

Children of James Tull Carey and wife Harriett Jane Walls (1845-1915) were Willard M. Carey, (1866-1959), Louis James Carey (1868-1943), Charles E. Carey (1869-1948, Frederic Carey (1873-1907), Joseph H. Carey (1878-1921), and Alfred H Carey, Sr. (1884-1932).

Information about a third Carey blood line in Milton, DE, was provided by a surviving collateral descendant of Jim Carey. He spoke by phone (March 2019) to my husband Niel Carey, pointing out that there had been an additional Carey family in Milton, including one Frank Carey. Relevant information about Frank was limited, but he mentioned Frank's important contribution over many years as a volunteer in his church in Milton when he himself was a young man.

As a researcher the task of identification of Frank Carey's ancestry with only limited information was especially interesting… I had been given a name, was familiar with the Milton location, and had about a hundred year span in which to search. Within a few hours I found Frank Carey and his direct ancestral line, but his lack of children eliminated a direct line of descendents.

Based on a calculated guess I found Frank B. Carey in the 1880 Census living as a 6-year old in the household of his grandfather, Joseph L. Black, shipbuilder, with his 29-year old mother Hannah J. Carey and other members of the Black family.

Who and where was his father? I found his mother's marriage record in 1916 (at age 64 to James F. Carey), referred to as her second marriage, which in itself encouraged me to keep looking for #1 and Frank's father. Also, the 1910 census had showed her as widowed. Further search revealed a 1871 marriage record of Hannah to Arthur C. Carey, born 1845.

WWI Draft records identify Frank as Frank Black Carey. Other census records identified his paternal grandparents as James and Elizabeth (Lizzie) Carey, living near Milton in Sussex County. In 1870 Census both Arthur and his father were shown as sailors. It was determined from his tombstone that Arthur died in 1879, but a cause of death remains un-known. Arthur and wife Hannah share a tombstone in the Goshen Cemetery in Milton.

Other research revealed that Frank, born in Philadelphia, had married Margaret P.Wilson in 1896, was without children, and had lived on Milton's Federal St. at one time. Censuses showed a variety of work experiences in Milton, i.e., Merchant, Furniture Salesman, Bank Teller, etc. He died in 1941 in Miami, Dade Co., FL, and his wife Margaret , six months later.

An obituary on a web site associated with Milton's historic Goshen Cemetery included many years as member of Milton Board of Education and his interest in civic affairs. He had been Grace Methodist Church's Superintendent of Sunday School for 16 years but resigned when he moved to Florida for employment with Apre (sic) Bros. Canning Company (about 1936). The clue about Frank was key to recognition of Frank, i.e., his having made a positive contribution to the Milton com-munity.

Finally, the previous paragraphs provide an example of the skills developed over years of family history research which have allowed me to give an identity to a person or people about whom I may have limited information — on this occasion with the use of my computer, Ancestry with its sources, and some-times Google.

The experience is typically fulfilling but, that's not to say, can be made frustrating when 'brick walls' occur… That's when one moves on and perhaps comes back days, weeks, even years later when additional information becomes available.

In retrospect it seems that about this time in my 'develop-ment' it can be 'off and running' in respect to family history research with one exception—that of having enough time for all in which I have an interest. My responsibility as editor for the Carey/Cary newsletter added a challenge.

However, the creation of the Carey/Cary newsletter was an interesting process, as I determined how I could use MS Word to creaste the newsletter, eventually with pictures. The publication of the newsletter continued for about fourteen years before all existing issues were archived on the web site, www.careycary.org , thanks to Sean Gilson.

In addition, intertwined among the research of various family lines for both Niel and me have been occasional *mini-research* projects for friends, relatives, other researchers. In those instances I supported their efforts, sometimes with limited research. The process seemed beneficial to them and interesting to me as I have had an opportunity to interact with others also interested in family history.

Finally, as a result of team work during years of family history research my experiences have been enjoyable, educational, beneficial, and broadening--hopefully for others as well as ourselves and our families!

CHAPTER 17

GOOD PROGRESS, NEXT STEPS
- E. NIEL CAREY -

The previous chapters have reflected the successful growth and accomplishments of the Carey/Cary Family organization over the past quarter century. During that time our Family group has organized with officers, constitution and by-laws, newsletter, website, and twenty five annual reunions. The leadership, active participation and support of family, friends and key organizations made this progress possible. As a result the Carey/Cary Family organization has members in nineteen states, from coast to coast, who share family research, often seek information about ancestors, and attend family reunions. For example, Rex and Janice Carey and Peggy and Kenneth Johnston from the Dallas, TX, area, have been active Carey/Cary Family members and have written chapters in this book. Cecily Hintzen, a family member from California, will share her Carey Family research in her chapter in this book and at the next Carey/Cary reunion.

As Rick Carey and I planned the first reunion, we followed my father's suggestion that we involve Carey's Church. Our subsequent contact with Ralph Dorey and Don Ward at Carey's Church proved to be, and continues to be, very helpful. Don and the Church leaders were enthusiastic about hosting Carey/Cary Family and the warm and cordial welcome from members, followed by a delicious meal, which altogether has become an important part of the Carey/Cary reunion.

As Helen and I have worked with Don and Anne Ward we have developed a meaningful friendship. Also our Family members have learned about the history of the Carey's Church and Camp and the spiritual service it provides to the community and the region. At the same time Carey's Church members have learned about the relationship between the Carey Family and Carey's Church. This is a prime example of the important and broader relationship between the family, the church and the community. As Don and I have worked together we discovered that we are related--through the Jones family. There is a lot of truth to my friend Lanny Rubin's comment that *"We are all cousins..."*

As the Carey/Cary Family became organized, with its officers and constitution and bylaws, it was decided that a means of communicating with its members and friends was needed, and a newsletter seemed to be the logical choice. Helen Carey became editor, manager and publisher of the *Carey/Cary Family News*. The newsletter has been an important means of communicating with family and friends--sharing information about family research and activities. However, when the CareyCary website was developed and became the primary communications tool, a collection of all newsletters--with the support of the Nabb Research Center staff--were bound and placed in key centers of genealogy research and data, including the Nabb Center, Duke University Library, the Maryland Historical Society, the public library at Carey, OH, and the LDS Family Research Center in Salt Lake City.

We were fortunate when Sean Gilson became a Carey/Cary Family member. He is a member of key genealogical societies and has successfully identified and researched his Carey family connections in Delmarva. He suggested that the Carey/ Cary Family organization consider establishing a Family website. Sean established the website, www.careycary. org, and even with increased work and family responsibilities, he has established and managed a important tool for communication of Carey/ Cary Family news and research. A complete set of the Carey/Cary newsletters are archived on the site, in addition to other information. Undoubtedly as a result of the website, individuals from

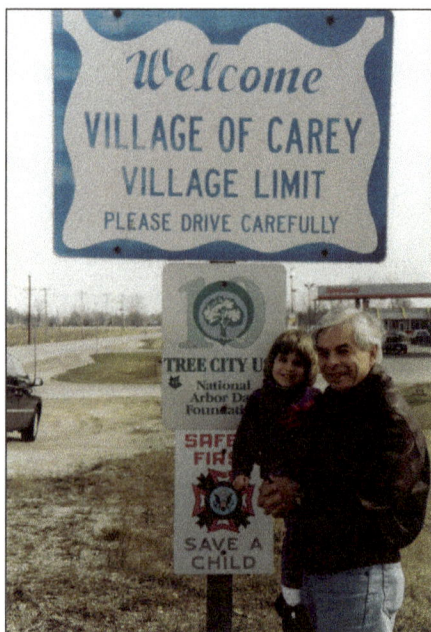

Niel and Carey McDonald at Carey, OH sign after delivering a bound set of Carey / Cary Newsletters to Cary, OH library

across the country became aware of our Carey/Cary Family and have communicated with us--sharing family research, asking questions and often becoming members of our organization.

Sean also helped our family organization become increasingly familiar with DNA testing and its importance as a valuable tool for family research. He is our DNA project director and has encouraged family members to consider a DNA test. He is also our family's contact with the international Carey DNA project. Sean's knowledge has enabled many of our members to benefit from this process, to strengthen their family ties, and to better understand their personal family genealogy.

Some years ago as Helen's interest in genealogy family research increased, she and I became aware of what is now the Nabb Research Center on Delmarva History and Culture. We were both impressed with the wide range of resources in the Nabb Center, as well as the Center's competent and helpful staff. For example, the Center has an extensive collection of records from Delaware, Maryland and Virginia, known as Delmarva. Helen was pleased that one visit to the Nabb Center could lessen a need to travel to two or more states to access archival records.

Over time Helen continued to use the Nabb Center resources in her Carey Family history research and I was invited to join the Nabb Center Board of Directors. I accepted the invitation and later chaired the committee which developed the first strategic plan for the Center. Also I later chaired the Nabb Center Board of Directors on two different occasions, and at the end of my terms of service, I was honored by the Board with the title of Board Member Emeritus. During my service on the Nabb Center Board, Helen and I supported and attended annual Nabb fund-raising events held at a historic properties on Delmarva and continue to do so as our schedule permits. We also endowed the Carey Family Research room in the Center.

There are several talented and dedicated members on the Nabb Center board. For example, Mike Hitch, current chair of the Nabb Board of Directors, has used GPS and related technology to identify and map the Carey family land grants in the vicinity of Carey's Church and in other parts of Sussex, Worcester and other Delmarva counties. He has conducted valuable family research and shared his techniques and findings at a Carey/Cary Family Reunion. His chapter in this book provides very interesting information about his family research as it relates to GPS.

When some of our family members suggested a more central location for our reunion, Dr. Ray Thompson, co-founder and later Director of the Nabb Center, offered to host our reunion at the Nabb Center. We accepted his invitation, and when Dr. Creston Long became Center Director, he extend-

Niel and Helen Carey Family

From the top: Noah and Aidan Webb; Christopher McDonald and Zachary Webb; Carey McDonald, Elizabeth Webb, Kathryn McDonald; Kevin McDonald and Rob Webb; Laura McDonald, Niel, Helen, Rebecca Webb

ed the welcome invitation. Respectively both have greeted our group with warmth and made presentations. Family members attending the reunion have had the opportunity to learn of the Nabb Center's resources and the Nabb Center staff members continue to be helpful and welcoming, Aaron Horner--a native of the area--is available to answer questions and provide research assistance and Donna Messick has provided an appropriate meeting facility with necessary technical equipment.

As Helen and I prepare to celebrate our sixty-first wedding anniversary we are pleased to support the publication of this book. It is a means of expressing our pleasure of being involved with the Carey/Cary Family organization and our appreciation to the Carey/Cary Family officers, members, friends and supporters of our Family. The book will permit us to have a permanent record of the success of our family group that can be shared share with our own family, various Carey/Cary family lines, and interested friends and neighbors!

Finally, we believe that families hold our communities and our society together. It is our hope that as we continue to work together, research, and share information about our families and their accomplishments, we will set the example and encourage others to do the same. Strong and active families will undoubtedly strengthen our communities and lead to a stronger and a compassionate society.

References

References
1. List of Carey/Cary reunion attendees 1994-2018
2. Carey/Cary Family Constitution

Attendees at the Carey/Cary Family Reunion 1994-2018
(These Carey/Cary Family members and friends attended one or more reunions)

Adams
  Judith
  Richard
Baker
  Vaughn
Barnes
  Edward
  Miles
Bergey
  Steve
Blevins
  Betty
  Ron
Bower
  Marian
Bracken
  Carolyn
  Richard
Brazaitis
  Edna

Breen
  Douglas
Bueg
  Sharon
Carey
  Alexander
  Alvin
  Anthony
  Asher
  Austin
  Barbara
  Bey
  Bill
  Charles
  David
  Diana
  Doris
  Dorothy
  Ed
  Ellie

Hase

Helen

Horace

Mak

Mary Alice

Mary Jane

Marlee

Nancy

Neill

Niel

Patrick

Pauline

Preston

Rebecca

Richard

Robert

Sally

Scott

Stephen

Stephen, Jr.

Sue

Susan

Teresa

Terri

Terry

Tonya

Vaughn

Carter

Dick

Cary

Jo

Rodger

Chavers

Cathy

Daniels

Shannon

Darwicki

Brian

Davis

Kathryn

Diehl

James

Dodson

Lee

Donovan

Don

Betty

Dougherty

Joe

Lottie

Fields

Jon

Linda

Fisher

Betty

Darrell

Fowler

Stephanie

Gardner

Gary

Jane

Garland

John

Mary

Gilson
  Sean
Grimes
  Carol
Hall
  Daniel
  Karen
Hanson
  Diane
Harrison
  Virginia
Hastings
  Ina
Herndon
  Shirley
Hill
  Kathryn
  Kitty
Hitch
  Mike
Hocker
  Carey
  Maryn
Horner
  Aaron
Howard
  Ellen
Johnston
  Kenneth
  Peggy

Joyce
  Carol
  Jim
Karl
  Tonya
Kenerly
  Michelle
Kotchenreuter
  Jocelyn
  Robin
Law
  Don
  Jacque
Leamy
  Don
  Marian
LiPuma
  Annemarie
  Joseph
Long
  Creston
Masche
  Jean
Masten
  Dan
McCarry
  John
  Virginia
  Timothy

McDonald
  Carey
  Christopher
  Kathryn
  Laura
Meade
  Linda
Messick
  Donna
  Jean
Monroe
  Jim
  Marty
  Oneida
Moser
  Lovel
Muser
Laural
Nelson
  Ralph
  Robert
  Sally Ann
Nichols
  Alexander
  Diana
  Gerry
  Lance
  Riana
Payne
  Harvey
  Mary

Pfotzer
  John
Philbrick
  Winfred
Phillips
  Barbara
  Bryan
Pierre
  Edith
Pullins
  Jan
Quillen
  Sandy
Richardson
  Carol
Ridgely
  Carol
Rorke
  Vicki
Ross
  Franklin
  Helen
Sherkey
  Margaret
Stewart
  Cary
Summers
  Tom
Swift
  Charles

Taylor
  Leroy
  Roberta
Thompson
  Ray
Trader
  James
Van Allen
  Carldine
Vanderwende
  Kim
Ward
  Anne
  Don
Warren
  Anne
  Ashley
  Bonnie
  Brent
  Elton
  Jessica
  Mia
  Rick
  Rochelle
  Sarah

Weiant
  Erma
  Richard
Wells
  Lida
Wharen
  Jeffrey
Wilson
  H. G.
  Pansy

Carey/Cary Family members and friends from Arizona, California, Delaware, Florida, Georgia, Indiana, Maryland, Massachusetts, Minnesota, Nebraska, New Mexico, New York, North Carolina, Ohio, Pennsylvania, South Carolina, Tennessee, Texas, and Washington have attended the Carey/ Cary Family reunions.

CAREY/CARY FAMILY CONSTITUTION

Article 1. Name

The name of the organization is the CAREY/CARY FAMILY.

Article 2. Purpose

The purposes of the CAREY/CARY FAMILY organization shall be to:

1. increase interaction and strengthen ties among members of the Carey/Cary family;

2. collect and share current, historical and genealogical information about the CAREY/CARY FAMILY; and

3. provide opportunities for interaction and communication with members of the family.

Article 3. Membership

Membership in the Carey/Cary Family shall be open to members of the Carey/Cary family, to those interested in the Carey/Cary family, and to those interested is supporting the Carey/Cary family and this organization. Members of the organization who have paid current dues are voting members. When members attain the age of 85, they will be granted honorary membership status, with full membership privileges. Honorary members will not be required to pay annual dues. A one year complimentary family membership will be extended to members' children when they marry.

Article 4. Officers and their Ejection

Section 1. Officers. The officers of this organization shall be president, vice president, secretary, and treasurer. Officers must be voting members of the organization.

Section 2. Election. The officers shall be elected annually by the voting members of the organization,

with the election conducted at the annual family reunion.

Section 3. Term of Office. The term of office shall be one year and until a successor has been elected.

Officers may be re-elected.

Article 5. Meetings

Section 1. Annual meeting. An annual meeting of the members shall be conducted at the time of the annual family reunion. Unless decided otherwise by the voting members, the annual meeting and reunion shall be held on the weekend following Labor Day.

Section 2. Special meetings. Special meetings may be called by the president, by any two officers, or by petition to the president signed by ten or more voting members.

Section 3. Quorum and procedure. Those members present at any annual or special meeting shall constitute a quorum, and the meetings shall be conducted in accordance with Roberts' Rules of Order.

Section 4. Notice of meetings. Notices of meetings will be included in the CAREY/CARY FAMILY newsletter, and mailed at least thirty days prior to the meeting date.

Section 5. Amendments. This constitution may be amended by a vote of two-thirds of the voting members present at an annual or special meeting of the organization

BY-LAWS

Article 1. Dues.

The annual dues of the Carey/Cary Family organization

shall be $10. Honorary members are not required to pay annual dues.

Article 2. Newsletter.

A CAREY/CARY FAMILY newsletter (CAREY/CARY FAMILY NEWS) shall be published and distributed on a regular (at least once a year) basis, to be distributed to family members and other interested persons. The president of the organization shall appoint a newsletter editor and provide guidance and direction to that person.

Article 3. Committees.

In order to carry out the organization's goals and to provide opportunities for members to be actively involved in the organization, the following committees are designated. Unless otherwise indicated, the president of the organization will name the chair of the committee, and committee chair will select the members of their committee.

Section 1. Reunion Committee. This committee, chaired by the vice-president of the organization, will be responsible for planning the annual family reunion, and for making arrangements for that activity.

Section 2. Archives Committee. This committee shall be responsible for maintaining the vital records and files of the organization, including minutes of meetings and treasurer's and committee reports, copies of newsletters, and other information needed to preserve the records and traditions of the CAREY/CARY FAMILY.

Section 3. Genealogy Committee. This committee shall be responsible for encouraging and conducting genealogical research related to the Carey/Cary family and for sharing and communicating genealogical information with the members of the Carey/Cary Family and other interested persons.

Article 4. Amendments.

These by-laws may be amended by a majority of the voting members at an annual or special meeting of the organization.

APPROVED, ADOPTED AND SIGNED:
September 9, 1995
E. Niel Carey, President
Helen Simmons Carey, Secretary/Treasurer

REVISED, ADOPTED AND SIGNED:
October 24, 1998
E. Niel Carey, President
Margaret Carey Sherkey, Secretary